This Land Was Made for You and Me

The Life & Songs of Woody Guthrie

"Woody spent his life, like a lot of us, searching for things to love. A little guy sloping down a dusty road, looking for something he couldn't name."

—Millard Lampell,
friend and member of the Almanac Singers

This Land Was Made for You and Me

The Life & Songs of Woody Guthrie

Elizabeth Partridge

VIKING

To my music man, Tom Ratcliff

03685903

VIKING
Published by the Penguin Group
Penguin Putnam Books for Young Readers, 345 Hudson Street, New York, New York 10014, U.S.A.

Penguin Books Ltd, Registered Offices: Harmondsworth, Middlesex, England

Published in 2002 by Viking, a division of Penguin Putnam Books for Young Readers.

2   3   4   5   6   7   8   9   10

Text copyright © Elizabeth Partridge, 2002

LIBRARY OF CONGRESS CATALOGING-IN-PUBLICATION DATA
Partridge, Elizabeth.
This land was made for you and me : the life and songs of Woody Guthrie / Elizabeth Partridge.
p.   cm.
Includes bibliographical references and index.
Summary: A biography of Woody Guthrie, a singer who wrote over 3,000 folk songs
And ballads as he traveled around the United States, including "This Land is Your Land"
And "So Long It's Been Good to Know Yuh."
ISBN 0-670-03535-1
Guthrie, Woody 1912-1967—Juvenile literature. 2. Folk singers—United States—
Biography—Juvenile literature. [1.Guthrie, Woody 1912-1967. 2. Singers. 3. Folk music.] I. Title.
ML3930.G88 P37 2001   782.42162'13'0092—dc21   [B]   2001046770
Printed in Singapore / Set in Caslon

Book design by Edward Miller

Picture credits and permissions appear on the last page.
Title page photo: Migrant workers forced out of Los Angeles by police activity, 1936

Contents

Preface
Rambling 'Round

"I hate a song that makes you think that you're not any good. I hate a song that makes you think you are just born to lose. I am out to fight those kind of songs to my very last breath of air and my last drop of blood."

Woody Guthrie could never cure himself of wandering off. One minute he'd be there, the next he'd be gone, vanishing without a word to anyone, abandoning those he loved best. He'd throw on a few extra shirts, one on top of the other, sling his guitar over his shoulder, and hit the road. He'd stick out his thumb and hitchhike, swing onto moving freight trains, and hunker down with other traveling men in flophouses, hobo jungles, and Hoovervilles across Depression America.

He moved restlessly from state to state, soaking up songs: work songs, mountain and cowboy songs, sea chanteys, songs from the southern chain gangs. He added them to the dozens he already knew from his childhood until he was bursting with American folk songs. Playing the guitar and singing, he started making up new ones: hard-bitten, rough-edged songs that told it like it was, full of anger and hardship and hope and love.

Woody said the best songs came to him when he was walking down a road. He always had fifteen or twenty songs running around in his mind, just waiting to be put together.

Woody visiting the Shafter Farm Workers Community near Los Angeles, 1941.

Sometimes he knew the words, but not the melody. Usually he'd borrow a tune that was already well known—the simpler the better. As he walked along, he tried to catch a good, easy song that people could sing the first time they heard it, remember, and sing again later.

Woody sang his songs the old-fashioned way, his voice droning and nasal, the words sharp and clear. Promoters and club owners wanted him to follow their tightly written scripts and sing the melodious, popular songs that were on the radio. Whenever they came at him with their hands full of cash, Woody ran the other way. "I had rather sound like the cab drivers cursing at one another, like the longshoremen yelling, like the cowhands whooping and like the lone wolf barking, than to sound like a slick, smooth tongued, oily lipped, show person."

Just after New Year's Day in 1940, Woody set off on one of his unannounced road trips. He left his wife and three kids in a shack in Texas and headed for New York City. It was a long, cold trip in the dead of winter, and every time he stopped in a diner he heard Irving Berlin's lush, sentimental song, "God Bless America," on the jukebox. It was exactly the kind of song Woody couldn't stand, romanticizing America, telling people not to worry, that God would take care of everything.

Woody thought there was plenty to worry about. The Great Depression, which had begun in 1929, was grinding on. For years, desperate, hungry people had been tramping the roads and riding the rails, looking for work or handouts. In Europe another world war was raging, threatening to pull America into the bloody conflict.

Bits of tunes and snatches of words swirled in Woody's mind, and a few weeks later in a cheap, fleabag hotel in New York City, his own song about America came together. Using an old Baptist tune for the melody, Woody wrote "This Land Is Your Land." His song caught the bittersweet contrasts of America: the beauty of our country, and the desperate strength of people making do in impossibly difficult times. Across the bottom of the sheet Woody wrote in his neat script, "All you can write is what you see," and put the song away.

Woody, on guitar, playing with his friend Pete Seeger around 1941.

Writing about what he saw—and felt, and heard about, and read about—gave Woody plenty of material. During his lifetime he wrote down more than three thousand songs, taking stories from everywhere: the front page of the newspaper; union meetings and busted-up strikes; and the sights and sounds of America as he walked "that ribbon of highway."

In April 1944 Woody recorded "This Land Is Your Land." When his good friend Pete Seeger heard the recording, he thought the song was one of Woody's weaker attempts. Too simple, thought Pete, an accomplished folksinger himself. Later he would say, "That shows how wrong you can be." Over the years he watched as "This Land Is Your Land" went from "one guitar picker to another," gathering momentum as it made its way across America and out into the world. After Woody's death in 1967, the song kept steadily spreading.

Today, "This Land Is Your Land" is sung all over the United States by just about everybody: schoolchildren, Scout troops, new immigrants, gospel choirs, and rest-home residents. More than half a century after Woody first recorded his song, Pete Seeger figures it has reached "hundreds of millions of people, maybe billions of people." Many Americans consider it our unofficial national anthem.

Woody would be proud. Years before he had written, "I am out to sing songs that'll prove to you that this is your world, no matter how hard it has run you down and rolled over you. I am out to sing the songs that will make you take pride in yourself."

Over and over again, he did just that.

Nora and Charley
Guthrie with their
first two children,
Clara and Roy, 1907.

Chapter One
1912 - 1919

Insane-Asylum Baby

"Don't you never break down and cry."

Some days Woody Guthrie's mother, Nora, could be wonderful—loving, gentle, singing and laughing, taking care of her family. But she had other days, too—days that were frightening and confusing to Woody while he was growing up. Sometimes Nora would pace around the house, scowling and muttering, or throw herself across her bed and cry for hours. Her trembling arms had a life of their own, suddenly snaking out from her body in rapid, jerky movements. For no reason, she could become enraged, shattering plates and cups against the wall, screaming at her family.

When Nora was calm, Woody listened carefully to the dark, tragic ballads she sang about lovers' quarrels, dying children, violent family feuds, and terrible natural disasters. To Woody, her songs seemed "long and sad, weary and dreary." But he listened anxiously, sure they held clues about what was making her so miserable. Was it the old house where they lived, with its damp walls and dirty cement floor? Could it be his father, Charley, out wheeling and dealing and fistfighting his way to the top? Maybe, Woody worried, it was something he had done.

Woody heard what the neighbors whispered to one another. They said when he was a baby something had happened to Nora. The doctor called it insanity and left it at that.

Woody's teenage uncle Warren was more brutal than the neighbors. After picking a fight with Woody, Warren screamed at him: "Whattaya know, you half-starved little runt. You done run yore mama crazy just bein' born! You dam little old insane-asylum baby!"

When Woody's mother, Nora, was growing up, no one suspected there was anything wrong with her. Born in Kansas in 1888, she moved with her family to a ranch outside of Welty, Oklahoma. The youngest of four girls, she was smart and energetic and loved to be outdoors working on the ranch. She rode horseback as well as any man, even though she had to ride sidesaddle like all women, with both legs on one side of the horse.

Throwing herself up on a blind gelding named Frank, she'd gallop between the scrub oak and blackjack trees, guiding him with her hands. Nora loved to sing as she rode along, going through dozens of songs and ballads her mother had taught her.

Nora was fifteen when she met Charley Guthrie. He'd been raised on a cattle ranch in northern Texas, but spent his evenings studying and learning. He taught himself bookkeeping and developed a fine, even handwriting. Like Nora, he'd grown up surrounded by music. In the evening after all the chores were done, his father played wild hoedown music on his fiddle.

When Charley was eighteen he left home and worked as a cowboy. But the work didn't suit him, and in his early twenties he took a job as a store clerk in Welty, where he met Nora. Charley was entranced with her. She wasn't silly and fawning the way many young women were taught to be. In fact, his brother Claude called her a "cowpuncher"—a seasoned, tough cowboy, capable of all of the rough chores and living a cowboy needed to do. Nora and Charley courted for about a year, then married on Valentine's Day, 1904.

During the evenings Charley continued to educate himself, reading law books, literature, anything he could get his hands on. In November 1904, Nora and Charley had their first child, Clara, followed by a son, Roy, in December 1906.

Oklahoma, known then as the Indian Territory, suited Charley. A wild, undisciplined place, the land had been set aside for the five "Civilized Tribes" after they were marched west on the Trail of Tears in 1838. The government assured the Indians that their new land would be theirs "as long as the grass shall grow and the waters shall run," but white land speculators, cattle barons, settlers, and railroad men all wanted a piece of the Indian Territory. In a bewildering series of land rushes, special sales, and backroom deals, they began grabbing the land. To complicate matters, whites fleeing from the law were safe in Oklahoma Territory, subject to neither the laws governing the United States nor tribal law.

Charley fit right into this wild, brawling place. A man of huge enthusiasms and contradictions, he was always ready for a game of poker, knew where to find the best homemade whiskey, and loved to settle disagreements with a fistfight. He earned the nickname "One-Punch" Charley for his fistfighting style: He'd grin while he fought, faking and jabbing with his left hand, then smash into his opponent's face with a lightning-quick right punch.

Charley (far left) working as a store clerk in Oklahoma, early 1900s.

In 1907 Oklahoma was granted statehood. With his book learning and fine, even handwriting, Charley was elected the first district court clerk of Okfuskee County.

Eager to celebrate his new position, Charley built a big house on a hill overlooking Okemah, Oklahoma, the new county seat. He painted the outside bright yellow and set up a study where he could relax and smoke his pipe, surrounded by shelves full of books. He bought Nora an organ she could play while she sang the songs she loved.

Charley's credit was good in any store in town, and Nora often took her two children shopping. She only had to sign her name in the store book, and Charley would pay later. But the townspeople noticed that Nora had some odd habits, like the way her arms flew out when she didn't mean for them to, knocking things off the shelves. Sometimes neighbors spoke to her when she was in town, and she didn't seem to notice them. At first people thought she was shy, or maybe stuck up.

In the fall of 1909, Charley and Nora's new house suddenly caught fire. The fire whistle wailed through town and across the farmlands. Everyone dropped what they were doing, grabbed buckets, and ran toward the column of smoke. Buckets flew hand to hand as people threw water onto the crackling fire. But the house quickly turned into a roaring tower of flames.

Nora stood on the sidelines, holding her trembling arms tight to her sides as the house burned to the ground. After an hour, all that was left was a pile of smoldering coals and the acrid, drifting smell of smoke.

For months afterward Nora talked about the fire. She seemed haunted by the loss of her beautiful house, her organ, and Charley's peaceful study. To make things worse, there was whispering around town that Nora had started the fire herself.

As soon as the family was settled in another house, Charley was back at the courthouse every day. Besides his official duties, he was soon in the land speculating business, selling, buying, and swapping land, filling out the paperwork at the courthouse. Speaking a little Creek and Cherokee, Charley was among the white men eager to "help" the Indians sell their land cheaply to cattle ranchers, farmers, and railroad men.

Clara and Roy Guthrie on the porch of their house, 1911.

African-Americans were also moving into the area. A few miles from Okemah was an all-black town, Boley. Like Okemah, Boley had about a thousand residents, from a small but steady stream of "Exodusters"—former slaves from the South looking for a place to settle in the West. Relations between the white and black towns were strained, occasionally flaring over into bitter violence.

Late one night in 1910, Charley was part of a mob that burst into the Okemah jail. A black family from Boley had been accused of letting a deputy bleed to death in the yard, shot by their son, Lawrence. The family was arrested, and the father locked alone in a cell. The mother, Laura, her newborn baby, and thirteen-year-old Lawrence were locked in another.

The mob overran the jail and dragged Laura, Lawrence, and the baby to a bridge spanning the nearby Canadian River.

Laura and her son were lynched, and the baby left crying beside the bridge where their bodies hung. The Okemah paper reported self-righteously, "It is generally thought the negroes got what would have been due them under due process of law." The paper ran a gruesome photo of the hanging bodies, which was later made into a postcard and sold in town.

Slipknot

woody Guthrie

Woody was appalled when his father told him all about the Okemah lynching. Years later he drew this sketch and wrote a song, "Don't Kill My Baby and My Son." He claimed in a foreword to the song that as he walked near the jail in Okemah he saw Laura "sticking her head through the jailhouse bars and moaning at the top of her voice."

On Sunday, July 14, 1912, Nora gave birth to another son. Charley and Nora named him Woodrow Wilson Guthrie in honor of the man who had just been nominated for president by the Democratic party. Charley wrote an article for the local paper, proclaiming himself "happy as a lobster."

Nora called her new son Woodrow, but everyone else called him Woody. As soon as he could talk he was full of questions, always on the move, climbing trees and fences, jumping and running around the house, making up rhymes and verses. Small for his age, he had wild, dark curly hair and a powerful stubborn streak. "You are my newest and my hardest-headed youngin'," Nora told him.

The first house Woody remembered was a big, dank place. The two large rooms on the ground floor were dug into the rocky side of a hill. Woody didn't like how the walls felt cold, and the house was damp and musty.

He could tell his mother didn't like the house either. Her songs were often melancholy, and her feelings easily hurt: The tiniest word of criticism from Charley and she'd rush upstairs and cry. And some days she wasn't able to do the simplest housekeeping tasks. Dishes fell from her shaking hands, and she sometimes lost her balance, lurching awkwardly as she walked from room to room.

Woody adored his sister, Clara, nearly eight years older than he was. Smart, sassy, and headstrong, Clara had long, curly brown hair. She was always dancing around, twisting, and whirling. As she walked to and from

Clara holding Woody, 1912.

school, she sang and skipped and ran. Full of spirit, she found it hard to sit still for more than a few minutes.

Roy, six years older than Woody, was quiet and thoughtful. Even when Woody saw him fight with other boys, he'd walk slowly into the house afterward and sit and think about what had happened, never saying a word. Woody admired his deep-thinking ways, and often stared at him, trying to figure out what was on his mind.

While Clara and Roy were at school, Woody listened to his mother singing as she washed their clothes, cooked, and cleaned. Charley also loved to sing, and Woody listened to them sing alone and together, their songs coming from all the cultures in and around Okemah. "The color of the songs was the Red Man, the Black Man and the White folks," Woody said later.

Woody heard so much singing that he began making up songs when he was very young. Standing in the yard one day watching Clara and Roy walk down the road to school, Woody decided the flowers and trees and pickets in the fence were his audience, and he made up his first song.

> Listen to the music.
> Music, music;
> Listen to the music,
> Music band.

The people in town continued to talk. Some had seen Nora galloping through town on a horse, not even properly sidesaddle, but riding like a man. She hadn't stopped to talk to anyone before wheeling the horse around and galloping home. And the way those kids were always dirty and hungry looking, it was a shame. She didn't care for them properly.

Charley didn't listen to the whispering. He'd announced he wasn't running for county clerk again, and was completely caught up in the land-trading business. Whenever he made money in a land swapping or selling deal, he bought presents for the kids. The yard was loaded with bikes and wagons for Clara, Roy, and Woody.

Things kept getting rougher in Charley's business. When he came home he'd often have new bruises and scrapes from fighting. Woody could see that his father had to "out-wit, outsmart, and outrun a pretty long string of people to have everything so nice."

All the fighting and outsmarting made Nora scared and worried. She begged Charley to get out of the land trading and swapping business. She wanted to settle down on a little farm and grow their own food. But Charley loved the brawling and swapping. He enjoyed outsmarting and outfighting people. Nora was terribly upset when he told her he wasn't going to quit.

Nora began singing her most melancholy ballads, songs of hurt and sorrow and suffering. "The songs were made deepest in me along these seasons," Woody said later. "This was the time that our singing got the saddest."

One night as Nora tucked him into bed, Woody asked her a question. He'd heard kids talking, and he wanted to know: Had she struck a match and set their big yellow house on fire?

Nora reached out and gently rubbed her trembling fingers across Woody's forehead. Then she stared at the wall, as if she was looking through it and up and over the rolling hills surrounding Okemah. Without a word she walked out of the room. Woody listened to her move around the kitchen, heard the splash of the water dipper as she took a drink. Then there was only silence, and he fell asleep with his question unanswered.

One day late in the summer Clara and Roy were back in school and Woody, still too young, was in the yard with Charley. The heat was terrible, the air fiery hot and completely still. Suddenly the wind started to pick up. It whipped along the ground, sending old papers, dust, chicken feathers, and pebbles flying through the air. Woody heard a low whining sound in the air around him.

Woody was so scared that he almost felt sick inside. He glanced toward the house. "I'm a-gonna run," he said to his father.

"Don't run," said Charley. "Don't ever run." The wind howled in faster, and a warm, thick rain began to fall.

Nora bolted out of the house and ran for the neighbors' storm cellar, yelling at them to hurry. Charley threw Woody up on his shoulders and pushed through the wind and

Woody sketched his father carrying him through the cyclone.

pelting rain toward the neighbors. Boards and trash and bushel baskets flew by Woody's head. As the wind howled around them, Charley dropped to his hands and knees and crawled, dragging Woody underneath him.

Neighbors' hands pulled Woody and his father into the cellar and slammed the door shut. Ten or twelve people were packed together in the pale light of a lantern. Woody scrambled into his mother's arms and begged her to sing "The Sherman Cyclone." Outside the winds moaned and rattled the heavy cellar doors, but Nora held Woody tight and sang:

> You could see the storm approaching
> And its cloud looked deathlike black
> And it was through
> Our little city
> That it left
> Its deathly track.

Hours later they threw open the doors of the storm cellar and found a cyclone had passed right over them. Their house was destroyed—the roof gone, the walls partly caved in. Every window was broken, torn out by the winds.

Charley was devastated, but Woody was secretly glad. Maybe his mother would be happier somewhere else.

But Nora's behavior only got more bizarre, her temper flaring violently out of control. Clara made her mother angry one day, and Nora chased her all over the house, trying to hit her with a broom. Sometimes when Charley brought meat home from the store, Nora would fling it out in the back yard for the dogs. Her flailing arms and lurching walk were almost continual now.

In February 1918, when Woody was five, Nora had another baby, George. But her care of him was erratic. A few weeks after he was born, Clara came home from school and heard his muffled cries. Her mother didn't seem to notice. When Clara asked where the baby was, her mother said he had gone away. Clara found him in the unlit oven, wrapped in newspapers.

Charley remained preoccupied with his business, leaving home every morning in a clean white shirt and tie. With land sales flourishing, he made enough money to buy one of the very first cars in Okfuskee County. Charley spared no expense, buying a car for the exorbitant price of $1,750.00 with "coal oil lights, high pressure casins, a squeeze honker, canvas top, straight fenders, copper radiator, lever action gear shift, and leather straps running everywhere to keep the top from blowing off."

Nora loved to drive the new car. She could get out to her mother's farm in a fraction of the time it took in a horse and buggy. And somehow she felt better at the farm. She was less worried, not so bothered by little things. She often took Woody out to visit her mother while Clara and Roy were in school. As Woody played or visited the animals in the barn, Nora spent hours playing the piano with trembling hands, singing her melancholy songs.

Grandma was painfully aware there was something wrong with her daughter and wanted to help. She insisted Nora see the doctor and tell him what was wrong, but he could only recommend that Nora rest and try not to worry. Grandma began bringing Woody out to her farm more often to give Nora a break.

One morning late in May 1919, Nora demanded that fourteen-year-old Clara stay home from school to help with the ironing. It didn't make any sense, and Clara insisted she had to go to school to take her year-end exams. Nora refused to let her go. They argued back and forth, yelling so loudly the neighbors could hear them.

Suddenly Clara burst out of the house screaming, her dress on fire. Terrified, she ran around and around the house. The wind fanned the flames, making them leap higher and higher. Nora appeared in the doorway and stood frozen. A neighbor ran after Clara with a blanket and smothered the flames.

From his real estate office Charley heard the fire whistle and saw people rushing toward his part of town. Sprinting out of his office, he ran past them and found his daughter, burned from her knees to her neck. Her charred skin hung in blackened, blistered chunks from her body. Charley fell to his knees and began sobbing.

Clara asked her father why he was crying, insisting she was all right. Burned so badly her nerve endings were destroyed, she couldn't feel any pain.

By the time Woody got home the house was full of shocked, weeping neighbors and friends. The smell of smoke and charred flesh hung in the air. Charley sat in the front room with his head in his hands, his face wet and puffy from crying. Woody slipped between people to his sister, lying on her bed.

"Hello there, old Mister Woodly," she said, using his pet name. Woody felt something drop away inside of him.

"Don't you cry," Clara said to him. "Promise me that you won't ever cry."

"I ain't a-cryin'," Woody replied bravely.

"I'm not bad off, Woodly," she said. "I'm gonna be up playing some more in a day or two."

Woody sat on Clara's bed trying not to stare at her burnt, blistered skin, forcing himself not to cry.

Clara turned her eyes to her teacher, standing next to the bed.

"Did I pass?" she asked.

"Yes, you passed," her teacher replied.

Woody watched Clara take two or three slow breaths, then her head rolled to one side and she was gone. Her teacher gently closed Clara's eyelids.

Woody kept his promise. He didn't cry. He held his tears in so hard they blinded him. He raced outside into the dark, cool night and ran around and around the house till he fell into his father's arms.

Chapter Two
1919-1929

Boomtown

"I guess I hoped too much when I was a kid."

Woody didn't break down and cry till he saw Clara laid out in a coffin with a glass lid. School was closed for the day, and everyone from in and around Okemah came to say good-bye.

After the funeral, the town buzzed with gossip. People remembered when the Guthrie's yellow house had mysteriously caught fire. Some said Clara's dress caught fire on the kerosene stove as she was ironing. Others whispered that Clara had set her own dress on fire, just to scare her mother. Still others blamed Nora, whispering that she had lit her daughter on fire in a fit of rage.

In the months that followed, Nora talked incessantly of Clara. If only she had let Clara go to school that day, instead of keeping her home to do the ironing. Clara would still be alive.

"It was too much of a load on my Mother's quieter nerves," Woody wrote. "She commenced to sing the sadder songs in a loster voice, to gaze out our window and to follow her songs out and up and over and away from it all, away over yonder in the minor keys."

In 1920, a year after Clara's death, Okemah suddenly became a "boomtown" when oil was discovered nearby. Okemah didn't have much oil, but the town's railroad station made it the major supply center for the area. Within weeks, carloads of lumber and drilling

Woody (far left) with his parents, Charley and Nora, and his little brother, George, around 1924.

A field worker probing an oil slush pit in Texas.

supplies were coming in on the trains, as well as thousands of men from all over the United States, looking for work in the oil fields.

Woody, now nine years old, loved the wild excitement in town. The dirt streets were full of horses, cars, and trucks. Mule teams pulled huge, overloaded wagons out to the oil fields. Okemah's wooden sidewalks were packed with rough, fast-living men out to spend their money as fast as they made it. Prostitution and gambling sprung up. The Monkey Oil Drug Store opened with a caged monkey by the front door. Prohibition made it illegal to sell any kind of alcohol, but bootleg joints like the Yellow Dog Saloon sold home-brewed beer and whiskey with impunity.

On the east side of town, tents and shacks of cheap wood and tar paper sprung up in the rough fields. The dusty streets often had brawling, drunken men settling disputes with blood-soaked fistfights. Several people were even murdered. The local police were unable to handle the lawlessness, and oldtimers decided they needed a vigilante force. A Ku Klux Klan chapter formed and Charley enthusiastically signed up.

In all this noisy chaos, Woody found ways to make a little money. He'd walk up Main Street selling newspapers, dodging out of the way of the bigger, rougher boys who claimed the best spots. Sometimes he'd gather his courage and toss his hat down on the sidewalk, singing the old, sad songs his mother had taught him, and new ones he was picking up from the boomers, like "Drunkard's Dream" and "It Was Sad When That Great Ship Went Down." Clapping and whistling, boomers would toss coins into his hat.

At night Woody dreamt that his mother was just like anybody else's. But she kept getting worse. One moment Nora would treat her children well, then something awful would come over her. Her face would twitch and her lips would draw up into a snarl. Spit would run out of her mouth and her arms would jerk uncontrollably. A screeching mutter would start in her throat and then build up until she was screaming, "God, I want to die! I want to die. Now! Now!" Then she would smash dishes and throw furniture around the house. When her fit had worn off, Woody would help straighten up the house before Charley got home. No one wanted to admit how bad things were.

In February 1922, two and a half years after Clara's death, Nora gave birth to another child, Mary Jo. Charley hoped the new baby girl would take Clara's place and ease the anguish in Nora's mind. But having a new baby only strained Nora's overloaded nerves to the breaking point.

Eager to be away from home as often as possible, Woody set up a gang house with a group of other ragtag boys: Colonel Martin, Thug Warner, and Casper Moore, a younger boy Woody nicknamed Tubbs because he was so chubby. By stealing old boards from a deserted house, they were able to built a tiny shack where they hung out during the day. Woody called it "Eeny House" because it was so small.

The gang spent days locking each other up in a jail made from an old piano crate, riding horses made from branches, and having serious, rock-throwing gang wars with other boys. When it got cold they dragged a big metal can inside, filled it with wood scraps, and made a fire.

Several times a week the gang went out with their burlap "junk sacks" to see what they could scrounge from the back alleys and junk heaps of Okemah. They collected old copper wire, smashed aluminum pots and pans, dented spittoons, old brass light fixtures, and scraps of iron and lead. The town junk man bought the metal from them for cash.

Never knowing what kind of mood his mother was in, Woody often wandered around

Woody sketched the gang house fights, calling these two "War Tank!" and "Hot Rocks!"

the east side of town rather than head home at supper time. One evening he came upon an oil worker sitting on his back steps singing while his wife fixed dinner. Woody threw himself down in the weeds and listened to him play his guitar and sing. Fascinated, Woody returned evening after evening to listen. Of all the songs the oil worker knew, Woody loved "Stewball" best.

> Stewbally is a good horse, he holds a high head,
> And the mane on his foretop is fine as silk thread.
> I rode him in England and rode him in Spain,
> And I never lost a dollar, I always did gain.

All the fast-moving money that rushed in with the oil boom should have created opportunities for Charley, but it only brought trouble. Business sharks swept into town and took over the land trading and buying business. Charley couldn't compete with these slick, high-stake operators. His business rapidly dwindled to nothing and he was forced to close his office.

Charley decided to sell fire extinguishers door-to-door. If there was one thing he knew well, it was the terrifying power of fire. Hadn't he lost a house and a daughter in terrible, consuming fires? But he was a poor salesman, and rarely sold the portable fire extinguishers. After he had worn out three pairs of shoes walking door-to-door, he quit.

Besides being dead broke, Charley was in terrible pain. Years of smashing his fists into his opponents had broken many of Charley's small, delicate hand bones. His hands were swollen and misshapen, and his thickened tendons pulled his fingers into his palms. One baby finger pulled in so tight that his nail cut a big hole in his palm.

When the pain became excruciating, he went to the doctor and had his finger cut off. In physical agony, with no good way to earn a living, Charley started drinking more heavily. He kept a fruit jar filled with bootleg whiskey under the front seat of the car. Woody would see him slip outside to take a swig from the jar every so often.

Charley decided the family needed a change. In late July 1923, when Woody was eleven, the family packed their possessions into an old Model T truck and moved to near-by Oklahoma City. Everybody found work. Woody delivered milk from a farm to the store for a dollar a week, Roy worked in a gas station, and Charley delivered groceries for a dollar a day. But carrying the heavy bags was excruciating on his broken-down hands.

At night Charley would beg Woody to massage his hands. Woody would rub Charley's fingers and palms. Feeling the hardened gristle and the tight, contracted tendons, Woody wanted to break down and cry, but he kept quiet. While Woody massaged, Charley asked him what he wanted to be when he grew up. "Just like you," Woody lied, "a good, good fighter."

Things didn't get better in Oklahoma City. Discouraged and overwhelmed, the family limped back to Okemah on July 14, 1924, Woody's twelfth birthday. They moved into a deserted two-room boomer shack on the east side with a little lean-to kitchen tacked on the back. From the first moment he saw the house, it depressed Woody. Dust blew in through the cracks, and rat manure piled up around gnawed-open holes in the walls. The whole place smelled musty and rotten, like an old sick cat had crawled under the house and died.

As soon as Woody had helped unload their belongings, he ran into town. He could see the oil boom had gone bust. People had packed up and moved on, following the oil fields that were opening up across Oklahoma and Texas. The monkey cage in front of the drugstore was empty and the sidewalks nearly deserted. The town had a melancholy, hollow feeling. But Woody didn't care. To him, the old alleys of his home town were better than anything the big city could offer.

After exploring Main Street, Woody ran home and threw himself onto the floor to play a game of war, using wooden matches for soldiers. Nora swooped down on him and took away the matches. She pulled the last match out of a crack in the floor.

"Maybe you don't even halfway guess the misery that goes through my mind every time I hold a match in my hand," Nora said.

She scratched the match across the floor and it burst into flame. Woody felt it light up both their thoughts and it "struck a million memories and ten million secrets that fire had turned to ashes between us."

Nora was glad to be back in Okemah. She started enthusiastically cleaning the house as soon as their belongings were in. Charley and Roy found work the first day, selling automobile licenses for the state. Nora was delighted, picturing all the good food she'd be able to buy. She smiled at Woody like she was "feeling a new light come back."

The next morning Woody jumped up early and took a shovel into the back yard, determined to plant a vegetable garden so he could sell cucumbers and green beans and watermelons. After he had worked for a few hours, Nora came out and took a turn with the shovel. Woody watched her digging in the garden. Not lying across her bed crying, not yelling or ranting and raving, but helping him out. "There was a feeling in me that I had been hunting for the bigger part of my life," Woody wrote later. "A wide open feeling that she was just like any other boy's mama."

But minutes later, something came over Nora. She headed for the house, and when Woody got in her way, she knocked him over with one heavy slap of her arm, her face cold and stiff. Woody ran all the way into town to get his father from his new job.

Woody's wide open feeling was destroyed. Leaving Okemah, coming back, nothing seemed to make his mother any better. Things weren't going to change.

But in Okemah Nora did find a place where she felt temporarily better. The Jewell movie theater on Main Street showed two movies every day. In the quiet darkness inside, Nora found some peace. She took two-year-old Mary Jo with her, and Woody would sometimes slip in and join her after school.

Woody loved sitting beside his mother in the dark theater watching silent Charlie Chaplin films. The funny little tramp with his wild mop of hair, his shy ways, and his messy clothes made his mother laugh, and Woody loved to hear his mother laughing.

Another big film star was Will Rogers, the Cowboy Philosopher. Besides films, Will was known for his fancy roping tricks, vaudeville acts, and weekly radio show. His tender, funny, boy-gets-girl pictures were a big hit in small-town theaters like the Jewell.

Will Rogers (in chaps and cowboy hat) on the set of his early silent film *Doubling for Romeo*.

Like many Oklahomans, Woody was an avid Will Rogers fan. Will had been born on a ranch in the Indian Territory in 1879 and was intensely proud of being part Cherokee. "My ancestors didn't come over on the *Mayflower*," Will liked to say, "they met the boat."

One day in 1926, while Nora sat watching a movie, Mary Jo wandered out of the theater. Charley found her walking alone down Main Street. In a flash of realization, he understood Nora was no longer capable of caring for Mary Jo. Stopping at home only long enough to throw her clothes in the car, he drove Mary Jo straight to his sister Maude's farm in Texas. A few months later when school ended, he sent George to Maude's on the train.

Unable to help his mother, afraid and unhappy to be around her, Woody was rarely home. For the next year he went to school sporadically, wandering around town unwashed and underfed, his dirty hair in tight curls.

Other kids in town thought Woody was strange and found ways to torment him. A group of older boys jumped him one day and pinned him to the ground. Despite his desperate struggles to pull free, they shaved his head with a straight razor. Woody was lucky he wasn't cut as the razor sliced through his hair.

One Saturday evening in June 1927, shortly before his fifteenth birthday, Woody was out at his grandmother's farm when the fire whistle began its long, lonesome howl. It made Woody anxious. He could tell by the whistle pattern that the fire was in his part of town. He went to bed that night wondering where the fire had struck and how much damage it had done. He could hear his grandmother in the next room, tossing and turning, worrying about the same thing.

The next morning Roy drove up to the farm in a cloud of dust and gave them the bad news. Once again, the fire whistle had been for their house. Charley had been lying on the sofa napping. Nora had walked over to him carrying a kerosene lamp, doused him with kerosene gas, and set him on fire.

Roy took Woody and Grandma back to the empty house.

"Where—how is Nora?" Grandma asked.

"She's on the westbound passenger train," Roy answered. "On her way to the insane asylum."

Nobody spoke. Way off in the distance Woody heard the mournful whistle of a fast-running train.

Charley was badly burned from his waist to his neck. In excruciating pain, he couldn't even sit up. After a few weeks in the makeshift clinic in Okemah, he was carried on a stretcher to the train station. One of the windows was pulled out of a passenger car, and Charley and his stretcher were loaded in through the opening. Woody stood on the platform as the train pulled out of the station, taking his father down to Maude's farm in Texas.

At first, Woody and Roy stayed in the house. Neither of them had the heart to cook, clean up, or wash their clothes. Melancholy feelings seemed to wash through the empty rooms. "That house, the kitchen so sour and lonesome—it seemed like everything in the world echoed there," Woody wrote later. "I had only one feeling toward it: I wanted to get the hell out." Roy got a room in town and offered to let Woody stay with him, but Woody headed for the gang house.

The summer was hot and wet, with rains pouring down and heat baking Okemah and the outlying fields. The gang could barely find a place to fish or swim. Escaping oil had found its way to the creeks, filling them with an iridescent black scum. Dead fish lay along the banks, rotting in the heat. The weeds turned brown and gray, and even the wild grapevines and tanglewood died.

Hungry and desperate for money, Woody grabbed his old junk sack and went scrounging in the back alleys and trash heaps around town. When his sack was full, he'd sell his load to the junk man. He stole watermelons and corn from the fields, and milk bottles off front porches after the milkman had passed by. Sometimes he would beg old goods from the bakery, or use his junking money for a hot, sweet-smelling loaf of bread. Some of the women in town took pity on Woody and would feed him meals of leftovers at their kitchen tables.

Rambling around town one day, Woody was passing the barbershop when he heard a man playing the harmonica. Woody was immediately mesmerized.

"That's the lonesomest piece of music I ever run into," he said. "Where in the world did you learn it?"

"I just lay here and listen to the railroad whistle," the man replied. "Whatever it say, I say too."

These kids are scavenging in a dump for usable items, as Woody did. Almost hidden in the garbage are two girls.

Woody began hanging out at the barbershop, listening to the man play the railroad blues. Before long, he was able to improvise his own version of railroad blues on the harmonica.

With all the bootleg beer and whiskey around Okemah, the gang decided to make a batch of their own home-brewed beer. The directions were to take one cake of yeast and let it ferment for three days. Woody and his friends figured if they used three cakes of yeast, it would ferment in a single day.

They hauled five gallons of water to the gang house and dumped in malt, hops, sugar, and three cakes of yeast. To speed up fermentation Woody made sure they kept a hot fire going next to the brew. Before long it was bubbling and foaming. After midnight they lugged a couple gallons to the school yard and drank as much as they could. Instead of getting drunk they all got so sick they wished they would just die and get it over with.

Okemah High School, 1926-27. Woody is sitting in the front row, fifth from the left.

Nights for Woody were hard and lonely. After the other kids went home to supper, Woody wrapped up in an old blanket and stuffed his junking sack under his head as a pillow. It rained and turned hot so many times that the fields seemed to steam in the heat. Water oozed out of the hill above the gang house, making the floor soggy and Woody's blanket mildewed and rotted. Soon Woody smelled of mold and rotten garbage and old trash. Lying in his old, damp blanket he'd have nightmares of demons and monsters and boa constrictors.

As winter came on and the weather turned colder, Woody's nights got even more miserable. Tubbs was especially worried about Woody. He begged and pestered his father to let Woody stay with them. Finally Mr. Moore said yes. The Moores didn't have much—eleven of them lived in a two-room shack—but they shared open-handedly with Woody. He squeezed into a twin bed with several of the other boys, sleeping head to foot.

Woody lived with the Moores for nearly a year. He let Mrs. Moore fuss over him, telling him to change his clothes and brush his hair. Living in a family where hot meals appeared regularly on the table and everyone behaved normally, Woody had a short burst of renewed interest in school. He'd get to class early and cover the blackboards with cartoon characters. He did well in two subjects: typing and geography. His teacher would let him type whatever he wanted when he finished his exercises, and Woody loved to let his mind run free.

In the fall of 1928, when Woody was sixteen, Mr. Moore began talking about moving to Arizona to find work. With the oil bust around Okemah, he couldn't get enough work to feed his family. Woody was welcome to go with them.

Woody didn't want to move west with the Moores. But before they left, there was something he needed to do. He asked Mrs. Moore to take him out to the state mental hospital to see his mother.

They drove the sixty miles to Norman, Oklahoma, and were let into the huge, brick building. Woody was taken down corridors and through locked doors that banged shut behind them. The halls and rooms were full of unwashed, broken people—muttering, wailing, staring, raving. Finally they came to his mother's room. She was wearing only a hospital gown, her arms flailing, her face twisting out of shape. She stared at Woody with no sign that she recognized him.

Woody stood next to his mother, unable to believe she didn't know him. Then, inexplicably, Nora's mind cleared. She looked at him and said flatly, "You're Woodrow." That was all, just, "You're Woodrow." Whatever Woody expected—to be hugged and fussed over, to know that she had missed him—didn't happen.

He stumbled out of the hospital, dazed and determined not to cry. But when he reached the car, he fell across the front bumper, sobbing deeply. Mrs. Moore held him in her arms while he cried and cried.

Soon the Moores moved to Arizona, and Woody was on his own again.

PAMPA, TEXAS

Chapter Three
1929-1935
Dusty Old Dust

"Us Okies are out of jobs, out of money, out of drinking whiskey, out of everything, except hope."

Charley had been in terrible shape when he arrived at Maude's farm. He lay flat on his back, weeping and smoking endless cigarettes. Maude refused to give in to his burns or his despair. She gathered sheep piles from the pasture, scorched them, and made poultices for the huge, open burn wound on his chest. After months of care, Charley's burn healed, leaving a thick shiny scar.

It was several years, however, before Charley felt like himself. He stayed at Maude's with his two youngest children, George and Mary Jo, regaining his strength and confidence. When he felt strong enough, he moved into nearby Pampa, Texas, leaving George and Mary Jo with Maude. Oil had been discovered around Pampa, and the south side of town was rapidly expanding, filling with pawnshops, all-night eating joints, pool halls and cheap accommodations. Charley quickly landed a job running a "cot house": a ramshackle building with a big, echoing room crammed full of cots downstairs, and hastily partitioned rooms upstairs.

Feeling independent and flush with his new job, Charley wrote Woody, inviting him to Pampa. Nothing was holding Woody in Okemah and he immediately hit the road, thumbing his way down to Texas. Woody was seventeen, but he seemed even younger. He

Woody in Pampa, Texas, 1931.

was small for his age, and skinny, with delicate features and a smooth, inquisitive face. When he walked into his father's little office at the cot house he felt painfully awkward. It had been two long years since Nora had thrown kerosene on his father and their family life had exploded. But soon Charley was showing Woody around and encouraging him to take correspondence courses and make something of himself, and the comfortable familiarity of their relationship slid back into place.

It was Woody's job at the cot house to show people "the right bed at night and the right door out next morning," he explained, "and to clean up rooms, collect rent, kill rats, and argue with roaches, bedbugs, flies, and ants which had a habit of living in our rooms without paying us rent." When he wasn't working, Woody sat in his father's office and drew India-ink cartoon figures and stuck them up in the windows.

Woody drew these sketches of a busy oil boomtown.

Shortly after Woody arrived in Pampa, on October 24, 1929, the stock market collapsed, setting in motion a tidal wave of economic disasters that began the Great Depression. People no longer had money to buy the goods coming out of American factories, and no way to pay their bills. Workers were laid off, businesses and farmers went bankrupt, and the economy trembled on the verge of collapse.

The oil flowing though Pampa kept the effects of the Depression from hitting right away. Stores stayed open, with plenty of merchandise for the boomers to buy.

Local businessmen saw Woody's cartoons at the cot house and hired him to paint advertisements. He painted signs on the sides of warehouses, barns, hotels, pawnshops and funeral homes. Merchants hired him to cover their plate-glass windows with lists of special prices and fancy holiday murals with turkeys, baskets of plenty, and Santa Clauses.

Woody used the money to buy tubes of oil paint, pieces of canvas, and expensive camel-hair brushes. He threw himself into oil painting, making copies of famous pictures like Whistler's Mother, then painting babies, boys with dogs, and landscapes of the vast, billowing wheat fields surrounding Pampa.

He also found a job working the counter at Shorty's Drugstore. Tired, thirsty boomers gave Woody a nickel to pull the handle on a barrel of root beer and draw off a mug of cold, frothy soda. And if they slid an extra fifty cents across the counter, Woody opened a hidden door under the counter, pulled out a two-ounce bottle, and poured the contents into their root beer. The bottle was full of "Jamaican Ginger," a rotgut, bootleg whiskey flavored with ginger.

Shorty could be raided and shut down at any moment, so he paid Woody cash at closing time. That was fine with Woody. He was taking life a day at a time anyway.

In the back room at Shorty's, Woody found an old guitar. When he wasn't busy serving root beer, he started figuring out how to play. He asked Charley's half-brother Jeff, who worked on the Pampa police force and was an incredible fiddle player, to teach him some chords. Jeff was a large, talkative man, full of enthusiasm for country music and get-rich schemes which never seemed to pan out. Widely known as one of the best fiddle players in the Texas panhandle, he could make music come whirring and howling out of his fiddle and was happy to show Woody how to play.

As soon as Woody had mastered the basic chords, he taught himself the melancholy ballads his mother used to sing, as well as songs he was hearing from the boomers, like "Greenback Dollar."

> I don't want your greenback dollar,
> I don't want your silver chains,
> All I want is your love, darling,
> Won't you take me back again.

One especially slow day at Shorty's, Woody decided to try the Jamaican Ginger. He snuck out one of the little bottles, poured it into a cold glass of root beer, and took a swig.

> It was hot and dry and gingery and spicey, and cloudy, and smooth, and windy and cold, and threatening rain or snow. I took another big swallow and my shirt come unbuttoned and my insides burnt like I was pouring myself full of home-made soapy dishwater. I drank it all down, and when I woke up I was out of a job.

While he was living with his father and working these part-time jobs, Woody made halfhearted attempts to finish high school. He'd enroll at the beginning of the semester, but before it ended, he'd often quit going to classes. Sometimes he'd manage to finish the semester, failing some classes, barely passing others. He preferred to sneak off to the library, where he followed his own passions, devouring books on whatever held his interest at the moment—art, psychology, even law.

Charley badgered Woody to stay in school, but Woody never compromised, doing only what he wanted to do. When his father got on his nerves, Woody would take a few bucks and rent a cheap hotel room, returning a few days later with no explanation of where he'd been or why.

While Woody was at school he met Matt Jennings, a tall, redheaded boy from a poor Irish Catholic family living on the south side. Matt and Woody had study hall together, where Matt watched in astonishment as Woody pulled a bottle of India ink and a brush out of his pocket and spent the period drawing instead of studying. Matt was fascinated by Woody—the way he'd ignore the rules if they didn't suit him, and how his mind was always turning and spinning on some new subject. But Matt didn't really get to know Woody until he bought an old mandolin at a pawnshop.

Eager to play, Matt asked Woody for his help. Woody—always confident of his skills—assured Matt he could tune the mandolin for him. But the mandolin was different from the guitar, and after a few frustrating hours, Woody finally gave up and took Matt over to Jeff's apartment. Jeff tuned up the mandolin, then whipped out some hoedowns, thrilling Matt.

Determined to become good musicians themselves, Woody and Matt began practicing together. They spent hours learning new songs and working on old favorites. Slowly they began to know each other without much talking, playing together easily, slipping into rhythms and cadences that brought out the best in their playing.

One day as he was walking down the street, Woody spotted a girl up ahead with long blonde hair falling down her back. He thought to himself, I'm going to marry that girl. He was astonished to discover she was Matt's younger sister, Mary Jennings.

The Jenningses were poor, but friendly, down-to-earth people. Once a week all the nearby relatives gathered at their house for cold cuts and home-brewed beer. Matt and Mary had something Woody had wanted as long as he could remember: a strong, stable family. Woody began spending as much time as he could at the Jenningses', practicing with Matt, flirting with Mary.

Weekends Woody and Matt went out on the town. Pampa was full of all kinds of entertainment designed to appeal to raucous, drunken crowds of unmarried men. One night Woody and Matt went over to the Playmore Auditorium to see a bear fight an old wrestler, Dutch Mantel. The bear had a muzzle and mitts on, but even so it cuffed and squeezed Dutch. The air was full of shouts and jeers, and the pungent smell of bear. To win the fight, Dutch snuck a handful of pepper into the ring and blew it into the bear's eyes. The enraged, blinded bear blundered out of the ring, terrifying everyone in the auditorium.

Another night Woody and Matt went out to the Red Barn to hear some country music. They had a great time together, listening to the music and gulping bootleg whiskey from a jar. Finally they stumbled back to the cheap hotel room Woody had rented and dropped onto their beds.

Woody never talked about his mother, Nora. Now, lying in the dark, he told Matt he had just received a letter forwarded from Okemah. It was from the officials at the insane asylum in Norman, Oklahoma. The letter was brief, saying they didn't know how to locate

A bewildered, muzzled and gloved bear in a boxing "match," 1938. Though the bears were strong, the boxer could easily hurt one by hitting its sensitive nose.

his father, but wanted to inform the family that Nora had recently died. A check was enclosed for $1.50, all that remained in her account.

Woody went on talking in the dark room. It was as if every one of his childhood memories was etched, sharply and painfully, in his mind. He told Matt about visiting his mother at the asylum, and how agonizing it was when she had barely recognized him. He repeated what the doctors knew: His mother had a hereditary disease called Huntington's Chorea. It was so rare, some doctors assumed it could only be passed from mother to daughter. Others thought any child—male or female—could inherit it from either parent.

But in Woody's drunken haze, he confidently assured Matt of one thing: There was no way he was going to get it. And Matt, full of whiskey, didn't ask Woody how he could be so sure.

A few days later, Woody took the check to the bank. As he stood in line, his throat was so dry he could barely swallow. When the teller put the money down on the counter, he felt like it took every muscle in his body to pick it up. And somewhere, on the outskirts of town, he thought he heard the mournful sound of a fire whistle blowing.

Woody was nineteen. He shoved his feelings far away where they wouldn't torment him, leaving only a desolate emptiness. Nora's death was a harsh end to any wild, unspoken hopes Woody may have had about his family miraculously coming back together again.

For Charley, Nora's death was both an ending, and a beginning. Now he was free to marry again. Charley wrote to a Lonely Hearts club and began corresponding with a woman in Los Angeles, Betty Jean McPherson, who soon agreed to marry him. In September 1931 she came from Los Angeles on the train.

Charley must have been surprised when she stepped off the train: Large and stocky, she had short-cropped brown hair and a tight, pinched face. They walked over to city hall and were married immediately and moved into a little house on the south side of town. Charley went right out to Maude's and picked up George and Mary Jo. Now that he was married, it was time he stopped relying on Maude to care for his children. They could live with him and their new mother.

Betty Jean was a disaster. She rarely bathed and had a fierce temper. When she got angry, she would hit George and Mary Jo. Much bigger than Charley, she would fly off the handle with him as well, sometimes ripping his clothes as he stood passively, never hitting back.

Woody didn't run into trouble with Betty Jean. Unlike everyone else, he found her fascinating. She did something she called "electromagnetic healing," a combination of laying on of hands and counseling. Dressed in a professional white uniform, she'd have clients wait in the parlor, then escort them into the back bedroom for one of her "electromagnetic" treatments. In exchange, they paid her with cash, eggs, butter, or clothing.

Like Woody, Betty Jean had a wide-ranging interest in the world: She was fascinated by Eastern religions, the Ouija board, phrenology, and palmistry. Off the top of her head she could quote several hundred healing scriptures from the Old and New Testaments of the Bible. To reassure a doubting client she might say, "They shall lay hands on the sick and they shall recover."

Something about Betty Jean was reassuring, and people believed she could make them better. Under her influence, Woody began hunting down new subjects at the library, checking out armloads of books on metaphysics, healing, yoga, and world religions.

By now, Woody and Matt were getting good at playing music together. With another friend, Cluster Baker, they formed the Corncob Trio, playing at ranches and wheat farms and square dances for three dollars a night. They modeled themselves after the Carter

The Corncob Trio: Matt Jennings, Woody, and Cluster Baker, 1931.

Family, who sang old-time ballads and gospel hymns with a tight harmony and beautiful, precise guitar playing. Woody made up new words to old tunes and sung them everywhere they went.

Between songs, Woody would talk in a slow drawl, telling jokes and entertaining the crowd. People found his understated humor wildly funny. He could even get laughs without talking. One of Matt's favorites was when Woody would go into a wild jig dance, unexpectedly freeze in a strange position, then start up the jig dance again.

Across America, times were getting tougher as the Depression deepened. Millions of Americans were unemployed, with no Social Security or unemployment insurance to fall back on. People stood in long lines just to get a bowl of soup and a cup of weak coffee. Homeless families camped out in parks, under highway overpasses and garbage dumps, or slept in their cars.

On Sunday nights Woody, along with countless other Americans, listened to Will Rogers's weekly radio show. Why was the Depression getting worse? What could be done? Will Rogers's attitudes made sense. He distrusted big business, bankers, and Wall Street, and always stuck up for farmers and hungry, unemployed people.

Listening to Will Rogers's soft, drawling voice was like listening to a wise and funny friend. Besides the familiar Oklahoman accent, Woody may have identified with Will in several ways. Like Woody, Will was a high school dropout, and though he had an obvious love of words and communicating, he hated formal education. When Will was only ten, his mother had died, leaving him with a lost, lonely feeling despite his success.

Besides his radio show, Will Rogers wrote a weekly column that was carried in newspapers across America. He slammed the Hoover-led government for being ineffectual. "You can't just let the people starve," he wrote, "so if you don't give 'em work, and you don't give 'em food, or money to buy it, why what are they to do? What's the matter with our country, anyway?" He proposed that the government hire the unemployed for huge public works programs and pay for the programs by taxing Americans with higher incomes.

Will Rogers (right, behind the microphone) introducing Franklin Roosevelt (far left) during the presidential campaign of 1932.

That's exactly what Franklin Roosevelt did when he became president in March 1933. Evoking emergency powers, Roosevelt passed the Emergency Banking Relief Act and set up programs to feed the hungry and create jobs for unemployed. To give people paid work, he started the Civilian Conservation Corps (CCC) and the Public Works Administration (PWA). Knowing how tough things were, Roosevelt even passed legislation allowing the sale of beer.

Will Rogers devoted his April 30 radio broadcast to Roosevelt, saying, "He swallowed our depression. He has inhaled fear and exhaled confidence." People felt that at last the government was making major efforts to help them.

Roosevelt's programs didn't exactly hit Pampa with a bang. Though people were optimistic that change was coming, life was pretty much the same. Matt's father was unemployed, and Matt was lucky to have a full-time job in a grocery store. Jeff was still working for the Pampa police force. Woody drifted between his father's house and cheap hotel rooms, loneliness gnawing at him. He began to seriously court Matt's fifteen-year-old sister, Mary. He liked her soft-spoken, gentle ways and her warm, close-knit family.

Mary found Woody fascinating. He brimmed with brilliant schemes and wild ideas. He drew constantly, put out a newsletter about what he and his friends were doing, and always had stacks of library books around. At any moment he would start talking about his latest interest. Whenever he had a little money he'd buy a notepad and jot down words to a song, setting it to a well-known tune like "Flapper Fannie's Last Ride" or "Gray Team of Horses." The Depression didn't seem to affect Woody as much as it did others. He just wasn't very interested in material things.

There were three movie theaters in Pampa, and Mary and Woody often went to the shows. Three days a week they could buy one ticket for thirty-five cents, and the second person would get in free. Some evenings they went from house to house, Woody and his friends playing music, the host families providing hot chocolate and cake.

Mary would rather be with Woody than go to school, and she talked her father into letting her drop out of high school. Woody and Mary began spending all their time together, and Woody asked her to marry him.

At first she said no. Her parents were adamantly opposed. They had a litany of good reasons: She was Catholic, he was not. He was four years older, without a real job, and no apparent interest in finding one. Once when Mary refused his repeated marriage proposal, he got angry. "You don't want to marry me because my mother died in an insane asylum!" he yelled. It was one of the few times he mentioned his mother to her.

But Woody wasn't easily deterred. When he went out of town to visit an aunt, he wrote Mary long, intense letters begging her to marry him. Months later, she finally agreed.

Mary and Woody shortly after they were married, 1933.
The photographer caught his own shadow in the picture.

On Saturday morning, October 28, 1933, Woody dressed carefully in corduroy pants and a nice shirt, and he and Mary walked over to the Holy Souls Catholic church. Woody was twenty-one, Mary just seventeen. Father Wanderly was shocked that they wanted to be married. Catholic girls were never supposed to marry non-Catholics. But Mary's mother had agreed to their being married and signed the license for her under-age daughter. The best the agitated priest could do was make Mary promise to raise her children as Catholics, and perform the wedding ceremony.

Woody and Mary moved into a tiny boomer shack with a living room, bedroom, and kitchen. They had only the bare necessities: a bed and dresser in the bedroom, a couch, table and chairs, and an old radio in the living room. Stacks of books from the library were everywhere. Woody loved to lie on the couch, smoking home-rolled ciga-rettes, dreaming and talking. He and Mary scraped by on the money he made playing music and painting signs.

One day Woody painted an ad on a grocery store window for the Cutty Hay Meat Company. A salesman coming though town took a picture of it and the company asked Woody to come and work for them. Woody turned them down flat. Mary was upset since they need-ed the money so badly, but Woody couldn't bear the thought of being stuck in one job.

It wasn't money or material comfort that Woody was interested in. After checking out all the library's books on psychology, he filled a notebook with his own thoughts on psychology and gave it to the librarian. She thought it was good enough to put on the shelf. He never told anyone else about what he had written, not even Matt Jennings.

Woody also developed a sudden, deep interest in religion, and insisted Mary go with him to services at the Church of God. Fascinated by Reverend McKensie's pulpit-thumping, fire-and-brimstone sermons, Woody asked to be baptized into the church and fervently studied the Bible with Reverend McKensie.

But it wasn't long before Woody felt that Reverend McKensie didn't have all the answers. He tried meeting with a group that went into trances. At home he burned incense and practiced meditation and yoga. He bought Kahlil Gibran's book *The Prophet*, and was delighted to find many of his own beliefs there. "The lust for comfort murders the passion of the soul," wrote Gibran. "Your daily life is your temple and your religion."

Still enamored with Betty Jean's work, Woody decided to open his own faith-healing business. He avidly read a five-volume set of books called *The Secret of the Ages* and had business cards printed up advertising "divine healings and consultations."

"All kinds of cars were parked around my little old shack," Woody wrote later. "People lost. People sick. People wondering. People hungry. People wanting work. People trying to get together and do something." Woody would ask questions until he uncovered what was really bothering them, then give them commonsense answers. He sprinkled his advice with biblical verses, such as "The prayer of faith shall save the sick," and Kahlil Gibran, "The deeper that sorrow carves into your being, the more joy you can contain."

People went away satisfied. Woody was discovering the power of words and how just the right words could have a profound impact on others.

With all of Woody's restless, inquisitive energy, an incredible pressure was building up inside him. For years he'd been voraciously taking in every idea and concept that caught his fancy. "Things was starting to stack up in my head," he wrote later. "I felt like I was going out of my wits if I didn't find some way of saying what I was thinking."

For hours at a time Woody typed furiously on his typewriter, writing an autobiography, making up stories, writing out songs. He sent short stories to *True Story* magazine—so many

Woody's sketch of his "trouble buster" business.

Mary lost count—but none of them were ever published. He'd buttonhole people, talking at them until they begged him to stop. Some mornings he'd set up his easel and paint until the light faded from the windows and he'd realize a whole day had gone by.

Of everything that caught his impassioned interest, music continued to be the most important. Whenever he could, he played in front of an audience. "Some people liked me, hated me, walked with me, walked over me, jeered me, cheered me, rooted me and hooted me and before long I was invited in and booted out of every public place of entertainment. But I decided that songs was a music and a language of all tongues."

Woody put together a typewritten book with fourteen of his songs, called *Alonzo M. Zilch's Own Collection of Original Songs and Ballads*. The songs were his first attempts to express some of his feelings in music. Many of the songs were simply new verses to well-known ballads, but a few had a tender simplicity that would become his hallmark. Woody had a way of catching people's sorrow and longing in a few simple words.

Despite Roosevelt's sweeping reforms, times continued to be tough across America. Things in Pampa, in the heart of the dust bowl, worsened drastically. The oil fields were dying out, and by 1935 there had been four years of drought. Strong winds blew across the high, dry plains of Kansas, Oklahoma, Arkansas, Texas, Colorado, and New Mexico, sucking up dust from the fields and blowing it thousands of miles away.

Families packed up a few belongings and headed for California. Highway 66, which ran just south of town, was full of "Okies" and "Arkies," their old cars and trucks piled high with their possessions. "We've been blown out," they said when they stopped to cook a meal by the side of the road.

Even when the wind wasn't blowing, a fine gritty layer of dust hung in the air. While Mary prepared dinner she kept the cooking pots covered, pulling off the lids only long enough to throw in ingredients and stir. She set the plates and cups upside down on the table. Just before serving the food, she flipped them over. Outside the sun filtered through a dusty haze, and at night the stars were muted and subdued.

When the wind blew hard, dust clouds would come billowing down on Pampa, driving the birds before them. Woody swore he could tell where the dust storm had started by the color of the cloud—black, gray, brown, or red.

On April 14, 1935, a huge dust storm blew up. "A whole bunch of us was standing just outside of town," said Woody. "We watched the dust storm come up like the red sea closing in on the Israel children. It got so black, when that thing hit we all run into the house."

Fourteen or fifteen people shoved into Woody and Mary's tiny living room, slamming the door shut behind them. The wind smashed against the house, throwing dirt and pebbles against the thin walls, forcing dust in around the loose-fitting windows and doors, and between the cracks in the wall. Dust hissed against the windows, darkening the room. Quickly, people threw wet rags over their mouths to breathe.

Outside, cows and pigs and chickens were dying, smothered by the dust being forced up their nostrils. The relentless winds blew dust into the house until Woody and his neighbors couldn't even see each other. Someone switched on the overhead lightbulb, but it just made a dim red glow like a cigarette. They sat in the dark, coughing and spitting out mud.

The fear in the room was thick as the dust. Maybe the winds would never stop blowing. Maybe they were all going to die. Many were ardent Christians and figured this was the end. God was finally wreaking His vengeance. Their voices muffled by the damp rags, people said to one another in the dark room, "So long, it's been good to know you."

Hours later the winds finally stopped blowing. Woody and Mary forced the door open and saw that Pampa was a sea of dust, rippling out forever like the ocean.

Pampa dug out from under the dust, but the afternoon spent in the dark, fear-filled room with everyone saying good-bye remained vivid in Woody's mind. Later he wrote a song about the storm that "dusted us over and dusted us under."

> So long, it's been good to know you,
> This dusty old dust is a-gettin' my home,
> and I've got to be drifting along.

And it wasn't long before Woody did just that, drifting away from Pampa, away from Mary, and the chafing constraints he felt in a little dried-up oil boomtown gone bust.

Above: Dust has nearly swallowed up this whole farm, but someone has hung out the clean wash to dry in the wind, 1938.

Left: A farmer and his sons run for shelter during a dust storm in Oklahoma, 1936.

Woody (far left) with the Junior Chamber of Commerce Band, Pampa, Texas, 1936.

Chapter Four
1935-1938
California and Lefty Lou

"Days tried to thumb a ride in a car. Night rode the freights
to make time. You hate to just sleep all night and not get
anywhere. You hate it even worse when a good hot meal is
waiting for you at the other end of the line and you ain't
had none in 3 days."

Woody didn't just up and leave Pampa for good. He started by taking short trips, first to East Texas to visit friends, and later back up to Oklahoma. He preferred to hitchhike rather than ride the rails, ever since a friend from Okemah had fallen under a moving train and had his legs sliced off by the heavy steel wheels.

Before he left, Woody wrapped his paintbrushes in an old scrap of fabric and stuck them in his back pocket, saying they were his "meal ticket." When he was hungry, he headed for the main street of the nearest little town, ducking in and out of stores offering to cover their windows with advertisements.

In Oklahoma, Woody dropped in on his brother Roy, working in Streetman's grocery store. Roy talked the owner into paying Woody to paint signs on the store truck. Woody painted "Here comes Streetman's" on the front, and "There Goes Streetman's" on the back. Everyone in town thought it was funny, except the owner.

Woody was home in November 1935 when Mary gave birth to their child, a girl. Betty Jean said the baby was going to be a very mysterious person, because she was born with part of the amniotic sac over her face. Mary didn't believe her.

Woody and Mary named their new daughter Gwendolyn, and called her Teeny. Fascinated by his tiny new daughter, Woody adapted a lyrical, tender song for her:

> She's my Curly Headed Baby,
> Used to sit on daddy's knee
> She's my Curly Headed Baby,
> Comes from sunny Tennessee.

But Woody would rather sing about Teeny than take care of her. He left that completely up to Mary. He started calling Mary "Mama" and was frustrated when she couldn't come watch him play music at night. The little shack reverberated with the noise of a baby crying at all hours, and Woody started itching to get on the road again.

When Teeny was a few months old, Charley's sister, Laura Guthrie Moore, invited Woody to visit her in Turlock, California. Grabbing his paintbrushes, Woody hit the road.

It was hard for Mary when Woody took off, leaving her alone with the new baby. She had no idea when he'd be back or if he'd be able to send money. But she knew she'd get by with her parents' help while he was gone. Besides, the roads were full of men out looking for work. Handbills littered the southwest, advertising jobs in the California fields. Maybe Woody would find something that suited him in California. There certainly wasn't anything steady in Pampa he was willing to do.

Woody headed west, thumbing rides with truck drivers, farmers, and families. It was the tail end of winter and bitterly cold. Tumbleweeds, loose gravel, and dirty, crushed snow piled up on the sides of Route 66. Often Woody'd walk for hours between rides, snow sinking into his shoes, cold winds cutting through his clothes, blowing grit into his eyes.

After a few miserable days of hitchhiking, Woody hopped a fast train in New Mexico. That night Woody was rolling toward California as the night temperature dropped.

Freezing winds whistled in through the open slats of the cattle car he was in. Woody and the other hobos in the car trotted back and forth in the manure on the floor until they were exhausted, then they made a big pile, one group of men sitting in the manure, another group sitting in their laps, a third group piled on their laps. "You didn't know who's," Woody wrote. "You couldn't see who's. You dam sure didn't care who's. You was just a grappling there in the dark—but there's a warm heat about a live human being that you are mighty thankful for when you've been out in the cold so long."

Woody was headed west at a bad time. Californians, afraid of the thousands of penniless Okies pouring into California, set up illegal roadblocks along the California border, turning back people who had no money. Men called "railroad bulls" patrolled the train yards with brass knuckles hidden in their fists and billy clubs swinging from their belts, kicking out drifters who tried to ride the rails.

Bulls beat up hobos, forced them to leave town, or had the cops throw them in jail on vagrancy charges. There were fourteen different "vag" charges the cops could stick on a hobo, sentencing him from a few days in jail to months of hard labor.

Inside the boxcars and in hobo camps a fierce, loyal camaraderie prevailed. People made "jungle stew," throwing whatever food they had into a metal can and cooking it over an open fire. Rabbits or birds could be roasted on a stick

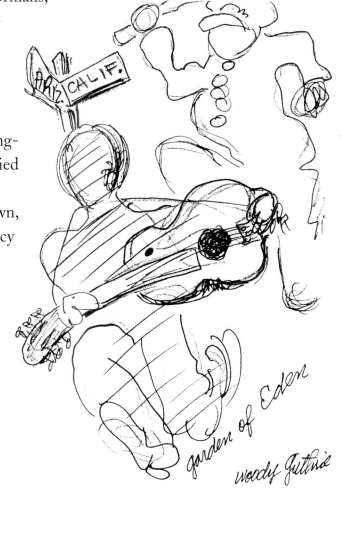

Woody drew this sketch of being chased back into Arizona from California.

Two migrant workers, known as fruit tramps, walking towards Los Angeles, 1937.

and torn apart with bare hands. After dinner one hobo might pull some coffee grounds out of his pocket, another an old candy bar or two. Though Woody often went hungry, he never starved. When he made a little money in town painting a sign, he'd buy food he could share with others, or give the money away to down-and-out people who looked like they needed it more than he did.

Staying at hobo camps along the way, Woody rode the rails into California, heading north through the San Joaquin Valley. Spring was coming, and Woody couldn't believe the intense greens of all the new foliage bursting out everywhere. It was almost painfully bright to look at after the drab grays and browns of the Dust Bowl. Even the air smelled moist and delicious and full of promise.

Woody spent several weeks in Turlock with his aunt Laura and her grown daughter Amalee. He was amazed by California. One man told him, "All you have got to do out in this country is just pour water around some roots, and yell 'Grapes!' and next morning the leaves are full grown and the grapes are hanging in big bunches, ready to pick!" California was so lush and fertile the story almost seemed true. At night the clear California sky shimmered with stars. Woody wrote Mary that California looked like heaven on earth.

But he saw other things that deeply upset him. Thousands of families were living under railroad bridges, near fields, or next to city dumps. They lived out of their cars or ragged shelters made of cardboard, brush, corrugated iron, and flattened orange crates.

Woody found that the handbills promising work for everybody were outrageous lies. For every job that was available in the fields, five or six people showed up and were turned away. With so many workers available, bosses dropped wages to unbelievable lows. "Take it or leave it," they said with a shrug. Entire families were forced to pick crops just to get enough money to buy food.

Everywhere signs were posted telling drifters to move on—they were unwelcome. Woody couldn't understand it. California could grow enough food to feed everybody—*more* than enough food to feed everybody—but the people who were working the crops were living by the side of the road, hungry, sick, and unwelcome.

Astonished by the bitterness and anger toward Okies, Woody headed back to Pampa after just a few weeks. He quickly settled into his old routines, working at odd jobs and staying up late at night playing music with Matt and writing.

When Mary told Woody she was pregnant again, Woody was delighted. He

Yakima Valley, Washington, 1939.

loved the idea of having another child, and went around telling their friends that Mary was "fragrant." Despite Mary's worry about needing more money, Woody didn't change his work habits.

Teeny had grown into an energetic, active toddler, and the little shack seemed smaller to Woody as he lay on the couch thinking and smoking. It wasn't long before he began dreaming about California, forgetting the anger, remembering only how green and lush it was. With another baby on the way and Mary constantly worrying about money, Woody felt like the walls of the little shack were squeezing in on him.

Another dusty, windblown spring came and Woody was more quiet and preoccupied than usual. Late one afternoon, just a few months before the baby was due, Woody suddenly jumped up off the couch and announced he was leaving for California. Mary was devastated. How could Woody leave her now, shortly before the baby was going to be born? She stood watching in shock as he pulled on a few extra shirts, slung his guitar over his shoulder, and took off.

Aunt Laura had moved to Los Angeles, and Woody hitchhiked out to stay with her. He found a job washing dishes in Strangler Luis's restaurant, but the best part of his day was playing music with another cousin, Jack Guthrie, who was living nearby. Jack made a living as a carpenter, but was an excellent guitar player with a smooth tenor voice. He had a reckless Old West way about him, cracking a bullwhip with such precision he could flick a cigarette out of a friend's mouth with a snap of his wrist. Woody and Jack began playing and harmonizing together. As they worked up a repertoire of songs, they tried to figure out how to break into the country music scene that was popping up all over Los Angeles.

Jack decided they should enter one of the singing cowboy contests at Gilmore Stadium. While hundreds of cheering fans filled the stands, cowboys rode in on their horses for the Grand Entry, then each group performed in high-heeled boots, ten-gallon hats, and fringed jackets.

Woody wasn't so sure about the idea, but Jack borrowed horses and they rode in on the Grand Entry. Suddenly Woody's horse bolted and galloped around the crowded stadium, spooking other horses and causing an uproar. Finally a mounted cowboy swept down on them and got Woody's horse under control. The audience thought it was hysterically funny, but Woody decided right then to find a better way to promote his musical career.

Woody and Jack wrangled a radio audition at KFVD, a station primarily known for its left-wing political commentary. The owner, a solid, white-haired man named Frank Burke, was passionately involved in California's liberal politics. He thought a cowboy show might attract more listeners to the station. On July 19, 1937, Jack and Woody opened with their first half-hour show at eight A.M. Frank didn't pay them, but Woody and Jack figured it was worth the exposure. They sang "Lonesome Road Blues," then harmonized on a few other songs, and Woody played backup guitar for Jack's solos. By September, the show was popular enough for Frank to put them on for a second half hour every day at eleven P.M.

As the show was debuting in Los Angeles, Mary gave birth in Pampa to their new baby, a girl she named Sue. Mary's parents were furious Woody didn't come back to see the new baby, and people in town whispered that Woody had left for good this time.

But Mary wasn't worried. Woody had made it on the radio, and KFVD airwaves were strong enough to reach Texas. She often stayed up late at night with her brother Matt to listen. Not allowed to say anything directly to Mary over the air, Woody dedicated songs to her and slipped in subtle jokes to let her know he was thinking of her and the two girls. When he wrote, he said he'd send for her as soon as he got the money. Mary hoped he'd have the money soon. She couldn't wait to leave Pampa and join him in the glamorous, showbiz life he was setting up in California.

A few weeks after starting the show, Woody asked Maxine Crissman, a friend of Jack's, to make a guest appearance on the show. Maxine was thin and elegant, always dressed in the latest style, and worked full-time in a dress factory for fourteen dollars a week. When Woody first met her at a party he thought she was one of the saddest-looking people he had ever seen. She was sick of working in the dress factory and didn't see how her life was ever going to change. But when people began singing at the party, Maxine came alive, her rich alto voice pouring out of her. Woody joined in, their voices weaving together beautifully in a natural two-part harmony.

Lefty Lou wearing chaps, 1937.

Woody was delighted to find that Maxine knew many of the same country ballads and folk songs he knew. Woody introduced her to the radio audience as "Lefty Lou from Ole Mizzoo. She's long winded and left-handed and she can jump a six-rail fence with a bucket of milk in each hand and never cause a ripple on the surface."

Lefty Lou made occasional appearances on the show until Jack quit, and Woody invited her to join him full-time. Lefty Lou was thrilled to leave her factory job. With the show gaining popularity, Frank paid them twenty dollars a week, which they split, going to the bank each week to cash the check for twenty silver dollars. The money didn't go far, but Woody sent what he could back to Mary.

In the morning, Lefty Lou and Woody drove into Los Angeles together, with Lefty Lou at the wheel. They ran through a few of the songs they would do on the show, but mostly they were quiet. It was one of Lefty Lou's great virtues for Woody. He had so many thoughts and ideas running through his head all the time it was a relief to be with someone who didn't fill the air with small talk.

In front of the microphones they sang folk songs, old ballads, and religious songs. Gradually Woody began singing his own songs, setting them to well-known tunes. He wrote up the lyrics so he and Lefty Lou wouldn't forget any of the words, and brought his songbook to the studio each day. Unable to read or write music, Woody memorized the tunes, occasionally jotting down which key they should be played in.

Between songs Woody talked to the audience in a down-home style like Will Rogers. He told tall tales, spun outrageous stories, and asked listeners about their experiences. Anybody out there ever see a hoop snake? Live through a cyclone? See a miracle happen? He invited them to send in their responses by letter.

One of the songs Woody wrote that he loved to sing was "Kiss My Mother Again."

> Dear Mother you're gone to your heavenly home
> Where heartaches can't enter in . . .
> Tonite all alone in spirit I've flown
> To kiss my mother again.

61

As he sang, his voice had a lonesome, melancholy feeling that moved his listeners. Hundreds of letters poured in, thanking Woody and Lefty Lou for their program, wishing them well, suggesting songs they'd like to hear.

But a few of the letters weren't so complimentary. In October 1937, Woody sang a song he called the "Nigger Blues." A black college student wrote in to say how offended he was. As soon as Woody received the letter, he apologized on the air.

"Folks," he said, "I got that song right here in my hand. Now you listen." Holding the page up near the microphone, he tore it in half and never sang it again.

The show was so popular, Frank added another time slot at two P.M., and raised their salary. They didn't have time to drive back home between the morning and afternoon shows, so Woody came up with all kinds of interesting places for them to visit: the zoo and library, bookstores and museums. At a used bookstore he found copies of the *Rubáiyát of Omar Khayyám,* a eleventh-century Persian poet, and Gibran's book *The Prophet,* which he avidly read to Lefty Lou on the lawn at the zoo.

Doing three shows a day, Woody and Lefty Lou quickly ran through the songs they knew and began hunting for new material. They performed more of Woody's songs, like "Talking Dust Bowl Blues" and "Do Re Mi," a common slang word for cash.

> California is a garden of Eden,
> It's a paradise to live in or see,
> But believe it or not,
> You won't find it so hot,
> If you ain't got the Do Re Mi.

Lefty Lou couldn't believe how fast Woody could turn an experience into a song. One morning they were driving in to do their show when another car came barreling down the street and smashed into them. By the time they had dealt with the driver, the car owner, and the police, and made it to the studio for their next program, Woody had a new song to sing: "Downtown Traffic Blues."

Another afternoon Woody was sitting on the porch playing his guitar when a boy asked him where he came from. "I was born in the Oklahoma Hills," Woody replied. It triggered an avalanche of memories, and by the eleven o'clock program he had the words to a new song.

> Way down yonder in the Indian Nation
> Riding my pony round the reservation
> In them Oklahoma Hills where I was born.

In December 1937, Frank offered Woody and Lefty Lou a contract. Woody typed up multiple versions of the "Corntract" and shoved them all under Frank's nose, begging him to sign them all.

With the radio show a firm commitment, Woody sent for Mary. Her parents didn't trust Woody and begged her not to go. She had never been out of Texas, had never ridden on a train. But Mary didn't care what her parents thought. Hadn't Woody made it on the radio? She couldn't wait to get to California and start a new life. Excited and scared, she bundled up two-year-old Teeny and the new baby, Sue, and got on a train headed for California.

Two days later she arrived at the train station in Los Angeles. Woody was nowhere in sight. Petrified, she sat in the station with the two little girls and no money in her pocket. What would she do if he didn't show up? Finally Woody arrived and took them straight to the beach, where Teeny terrified Mary by running right into the ocean.

They moved in with Woody's cousin Amalee, her husband, and their little children. The house was jammed full of Guthries day and night. Mary and Amalee became good friends, often starting a pot of beans in the morning and taking the kids to the beach and the zoo. In the evenings they made popcorn and stayed up late, playing poker and drinking red wine. Mary was thrilled to be in California. It was green and lush and Woody was on his way to being big, maybe really big, like Will Rogers. Mary figured she was out of the Dust Bowl for good.

It wasn't long before the crowded, noisy house and the demands of family life pressed in on Woody. Without any explanations to Mary, he began disappearing. He'd stay at Lefty Lou's after the afternoon program, painting in the garage or falling asleep on the living room floor. After the eleven o'clock program he sometimes didn't go home, but went out to the bars on San Fernando Avenue, singing and drinking.

Mary waited, anxious and impatient, not sure what was going on. Just then her brother Matt came into town for a visit and paired up with Lefty Lou. Mary's worries evaporated, and the whole Guthrie clan welcomed in New Year's Day 1938 at a restaurant after the show.

The radio program was so successful Woody and Lefty Lou were asked to do their show in Tijuana, Mexico, on station XELO. The transmitters at XELO were much more powerful than the transmitters in Los Angeles and the show could be broadcast throughout most of North America.

Despite their new contract at KFVD, Woody jumped at the chance. Maybe this was the big time they had been dreaming about. Woody talked Frank into letting them out of their contract, and by January 25, 1938, he was heading south with a group of musicians. Mary and the two girls came, Lefty Lou brought her parents, and Matt came along with his fiddle. They moved into a cheap motel in Chula Vista, just inside the American border, driving across the border into Tijuana to do their show.

From the very beginning the show was a disaster. The promoter, an obnoxious man named Hal Horton, tried to control their performances, telling them to be more professional and organized. Woody was furious. Nobody told him how to play his music. He and Hal had loud, angry fights, and after a few weeks Hal got the upper hand by refusing to pay them. Matt decided he'd had enough and headed back to Pampa. Woody and Lefty Lou limped back to Los Angeles with their families. They had no place to live, no jobs, and no money.

Frank Burke came to their rescue and hired them back, but it just wasn't the same. Woody and Lefty Lou were running out of enthusiasm. By June 1938 they called it quits. Lefty Lou moved north to Chico, California, with her family and Woody hopped a freight train, leaving Mary and the kids in an apartment in Los Angeles.

A group of musicians at radio station XELO in Mexico (1938). Lefty Lou is seated in the flowered dress, and Woody is lolling on the lower right.

Take it easy.
But take it.
Woody Guthrie.

Chapter Five
1938-1940

"Woody Sez"

"The best stuff you can sing about is what you saw and if you look hard enough you can see plenty to sing about."

After more than a year in Los Angeles, the freedom of being on the road again was incredible. But when Woody stopped over in a squalid migrant camp, his light, open feelings quickly plummeted. Some people had been living in the camps for several years now, barely scratching out a subsistence living. They were desperate, and angry.

In nearby orchards, growers hired armed guards to protect the ripe fruit while the migrant children's bellies swelled with hunger. When the migrants tried to scavenge leftover crops from piles on the ground, some growers poured kerosene over them, tossed on a match, and burnt them until they were charred and inedible.

Earnest young people—many of them Communists—began visiting the camps, urging the migrants to organize and form unions to protect themselves. Many were drawn to the American Communist Party—not only migrants, but workers across America. They were attracted to the ideals of an economic system in which the workers share the profits equally according to their needs. It sure looked better than the system they were working under.

The migrant workers set up strike headquarters and formed picket lines. The growers

Woody outside the office of the Communist newspaper *People's World* in Los Angeles, 1939.

swiftly struck back, hiring thugs to scatter the picket lines and drive suspected agitators out of town. Sometimes entire migrant camps were tear-gassed, shot at, or burned down, forcing the migrants to flee. Local police looked away, or even helped the growers.

After bumming around California for a few weeks, Woody was eager to get back on the radio and tell people about what he'd been seeing out in the camps and fields. But Frank Burke wasn't enthusiastic about having Woody do the radio show without Lefty Lou. It was the two of them together who had created the magic. Frank grudgingly let Woody have half an hour a day, at no pay.

Alarmed by the power of the big growers during the cotton strike, a gas station owner put this sign up by the air pump to encourage the striking workers.

Mary couldn't see how they were going to pay the rent. Woody, as usual, didn't share her fears. Somehow, they always managed to get by. He loved his children but wasn't burdened by a sense of responsibility for them. That fell squarely on Mary. Raising the kids on almost no money—and that money coming in irregularly—was wearing her down. And what about the career he was supposed to be building?

Whenever Mary tried to talk to Woody about it, he would explode and lash out at her, storming out of the house in the middle of a fight. It might be days before she would see him again.

As Woody moved restlessly around town, tramping along the roads and stopping in bars with his guitar, he wrote a melancholy song, "Left in This World All Alone," claiming he had no parents or friends, and that as he walked the streets he never saw a soul he knew. Woody often sang the song on his fall radio program. "I still feel this way a lot of my time," he admitted.

At the radio station, Woody started hanging around after his show to listen to Ed Robbins, whose program followed his. Ed was the Los Angeles editor for the *People's World*, a Communist newspaper. His radio show was a daily roundup of the news viewed from the "left," with a focus on workers' struggles and unions. Woody was eager to learn more about the Communist party.

While Communism looked like a good solution to Ed and thousands of others, members of the party were highly secretive about their membership. They could lose their jobs, be "blacklisted" so they couldn't get another good job, or even be beaten up by local police.

Woody asked Ed to listen to his show, and Ed liked what he heard. The man he'd assumed was just a "cowboy crooner" was singing and talking about the "damn bankers, the men that broke us and the dust that choked us." He was talking about the miserable conditions the migrants were enduring.

Ed invited Woody to sing at a rally. Not sure how politically naive Woody was, Ed felt compelled to add, "I would like you to know, Woody, that this is sponsored by the Communist party and it's a politically left-wing gathering."

"Left wing, right wing, chicken wing—it's the same thing to me," Woody replied. "I sing my songs wherever I can sing 'em."

At the rally, there were so many speakers that Woody, sitting on the stage, fell fast asleep. Well past eleven it was finally time for him to go on. Ed nudged him and Woody got up in front of the microphone. The audience was already standing and putting on their coats to go home. But once Woody started singing, he mesmerized them: Here was a real Okie, singing hard-hitting songs and telling funny, bitter stories.

After the show Woody went home with Ed, rolled up in a blanket, and fell asleep on the living room floor. In the morning Ed drove Woody home and was astonished to find that Woody had a wife and two kids. "Where ya been?" asked Mary when they walked into the house. "I ain't seen you for three days."

With Ed acting as his informal booking agent over the next year, Woody became a popular performer at local rallies, fund-raising parties, and union halls. He'd get paid a few dollars, which he might give away, spend on booze, or take home to Mary. Woody never refused a booking. Ed's biggest problem was getting Woody off the stage. He'd drawl out long, complex stories and seemed to have an endless supply of songs he wanted to sing.

A few months after the first rally, Woody dropped in at Ed's office to ask if he could write a column for Ed's paper, the *People's World*. As much as he loved Woody's performances, Ed was dubious that an uneducated man like Woody would be able to write a good column. He cautiously replied, "I'd like to see some and then I'll see what I can do."

To Ed's astonishment, Woody reached into his pockets and pulled out twenty or thirty sheets of paper. He'd already written a number of columns, each with its own cartoon illustrations. Ed was impressed. He contacted the head editor of the paper, who was delighted by what Woody had done and began running the column, titled "Woody Sez."

Like Will Rogers, Woody wrote in an easy, low-key style about the Okies, Skid Row, politics, war, and music. Sometimes his column wandered and seemed pointless, but other times his words were sharp and focused, like his songs.

> Billionaires cause hoboes, and hoboes make billionaires. Yet both cuss the other and say they are wrong . . . but personal I ruther trust the hoboes. Most of what I know I learned from the kids and the hoboes. Kids first. Hoboes second. Rich folks last—and I don't give a dam if you like it or not.

Though he was writing a column in a Communist newspaper and often performed at Communist meetings, Woody never admitted to being a member of the party. He was probably considered too erratic and undisciplined by top party leaders to be asked to join. Members had to attend regular study groups, and Woody had no patience for sitting around being talked at. He didn't listen long to other people before he wanted to be the one doing the talking and singing.

One hot day in July 1939, Ed introduced Woody to Will Geer, a tall, gregarious man who loved to garden and memorized a poem a day for the sheer pleasure of it. Respected as a Shakespearean actor, Will was at his most expansive up on a makeshift stage in front of a group of workers. Accompanied by a ballad singer he'd act out the lyrics in broad, overly simplified moves, then recite tender, evocative poetry. He encouraged people to join fledgling unions and fight for their rights. Like Woody, he was too eccentric to be an official member of the Communist party, but was considered a "fellow traveler," holding many of the Communist ideals.

Will invited Woody to perform with him and his wife, Herta, at one of the new migrant camps set up by the government. For several years the Farm Security Administration had been sending photographers such as Dorothea Lange and Russell Lee into the Central Valley. When Congress saw pictures of the migrants' miserable living conditions, they allocated money for more than twenty temporary camps with tents, running water, and bathrooms. The camps only had room for a fraction of the homeless migrants, but it was a start.

In the middle of each camp was a large, high-ceiling building used for meetings and church services. Saturday nights the exhausted migrants filled the building for entertainment. Herta and Will made up skits to go with several of Woody's songs, including "Do Re Mi." Will recited poems, and Woody sang and told stories. The audience roared with laughter when he explained what he was doing in California: "Just traveling around, looking for my family. Forgot which railroad bridge they're camped under."

They started making regular weekend trips to the camps. Everywhere they went, Woody listened to people singing a religious tune popularized by his old idols, the Carter Family, "This World Is Not My Home."

This world is not my home
I'm just a-passing through
My treasures and hopes are all beyond the blue
Where many Christian children
Have gone on before
And I can't feel at home in this world anymore.

Woody didn't like the message—that the migrants needed to be meek and patient and wait for their reward in the afterlife.

As he saw how most of the migrants "lived outside like coyotes, around in the trees and timber and under the bridges along all the railroad tracks and in their little shack houses that they built out of cardboard and tow sacks and old corrugated iron that they got out of the dumps, it just struck me to write this song that 'I Ain't Got No Home in the World Anymore.'"

I ain't got no home,
I'm just a-rambling round
I work when I can get it,
I go from town to town.

The verses continued, each one hard-hitting: "Rich men took my home and drove me from my door / My wife took down and died upon the cabin floor."

In the camps and on the radio, Woody was singing it like he was seeing it.

I spoke out for equal rights for all races of people, Hindu, Japanese, Chinese, Okies, Arkies, Texans, Dust Bowl Refugees, and Migratory Workers. I cussed out high rents, robbing landlords, and loan sharks, finance companies, and punk politicians in all offices.

A boy finds plenty of time to practice his guitar while his family is stalled out in "Rambler's Park," 1939.

Woody was a huge success with the migrants. The anger in his words resonated with the rage they felt inside, and the sad, lonely quality in his voice echoed their experience in California. As he sang, they jumped to their feet, clapping, whistling, and cheering.

> So we drove all over the mountains and deserts in my $45
> 1931 Chevrolet until it finally shook completely to pieces. We
> saw lots of the Vigilante (Deputy Thug) Patrolmen at work
> with their brass knucks, billies, hoses, lead pipes, axe and pick
> handles, and sawed off shot guns, as well as gas bombs, and
> sub machine guns turned against the working people in order
> to try to make them work cheaper.

Being back in the camps was a huge turning point in Woody's life. Out in the fields of America, the Land of Plenty, people were starving. He had a vision of a world where everybody had a home and enough to eat. If people would work together, he was sure they could make their lives better. Woody was ready to use his music to point out how bad things were, and to change things.

Will was amazed by Woody. He watched as new songs burst out of Woody, several a week, sometimes a new song every day. Will realized how arrogant he had been about his ability to memorize a poem a day. Now he saw that he was just taking someone else's words and saying them to himself over and over. Woody was creating something new every day.

Will began taking Woody to perform at Hollywood parties. He asked Mary, pregnant again, to have a small role in a movie he was starring in about a country doctor who shows women how to safely deliver their children at home. Will's wife, Herta, was pregnant at the same time, and they played the doctor's patients.

Mary was relieved things were on an upswing again. Woody was talented, sought after, and getting to know the right people. It made it easier for her to put up with his wandering ways and sporadic income. For the first time in months Mary let herself hope that their lives would get better.

On August 23, 1939, shocking news came from Europe. The Soviet Union and Germany had signed a nonaggression pact. Russia would remain neutral if Germany attacked other nations, and Germany agreed not to invade the Soviet Union.

Americans were stunned, including many staunch Communists. They couldn't believe Stalin, in the Soviet Union, would sign a treaty with Hitler in Germany. The Soviet Union was a Communist government. After overthrowing an oppressive tsar, Communists now ran the country "for the benefit of all the people." Hitler went against everything that Communists stood for. He was a fascist—a man in power by brute force, imposing his will on the German people.

The pact splintered the American Communist Party. Many people now realized that Stalinist Russia was actually a totalitarian system, capable of doing anything to further its own purposes. Frank Burke felt like he'd taken a sucker punch to the stomach. Others, like Woody, rationalized the pact, saying the Soviet Union had to protect itself somehow from the fascist threat of Hitler.

Less than two weeks later, Germany invaded western Poland, and Great Britain and France declared war on Germany. World War II had begun. Woody wrote to his sister Mary Jo:

> Now it looks like there are some wars breaking out around over the world. This is between the rich people. Us poor folks have nothing in the world to do with these wars, because, win, lose, or draw, we are poor to commence with and will be poor to end with. So it is plain that these wars are between the rich people, for more lands, more fields, more mines, more oil fields, more factories, more colonies, more folks to work for them, and more profits in their pockets.

Woody even seemed to take perverse pleasure in defending the Russian Communists now that they were suspect in many people's minds. One evening Mary asked him to take care of Sue and Teeny, now two and almost four years old, so she and Amalee could go to the movies. He refused, saying that in Russia the state provided baby-sitting. On the air, he defended Russia when their army swept into Poland. When Frank asked him to tone it down, Woody refused.

In early October things reached the boiling point in the cotton fields near Arvin, California. The pickers demanded higher wages, and the growers made a final offer of eighty cents for each hundred pounds of cotton they picked. The workers went out on strike, and the situation flared into violence. Hundreds of workers were arrested, and dozens beaten up.

Will and a group of Hollywood celebrities decided to add their clout to the workers' struggle, and set off for Arvin to perform for the weekend. Woody went with them, even though Mary was due to have the baby any moment and wanted him nearby. When he got back home several days later, he found Mary had given birth to their son, Will Rogers Guthrie.

Woody proudly announced the birth in his column.

> Special to The People's World: October 7. A big, long, tall, husky, loud, noisy 8 1/4 pound Baby Boy arrived at my house. Been a watchin him mighty close to see if he's a right-winger or a left-winger. Impossible to keep covers on him. Kicks worse then a millionaire getting taxed 2 cents.

Woody's support of Russia continued to erode his relationship with Frank. When the Russians invaded the small country of Finland in November, Frank could no longer tolerate Woody's pro-Russia stance. It was the end of his radio show on KFVD.

About this same time, Will Geer got an offer he couldn't refuse—the chance to play the lead role in *Tobacco Road* on Broadway. He and Herta moved to New York with their

Will Geer in 1941 as Jeeter Lester in *Tobacco Road*.

new baby, Katie. Woody kept performing on his own, but without the electricity of Will and Herta, his performances weren't as good, and he knew it.

Life was closing in on Woody again. Just before Thanksgiving he bought a used '29 Chevy sedan, packed up Mary and the three kids, and headed back to Texas. The engine block cracked, and exhaust fumes nearly choked them to death. But they made it back to Pampa and moved into the old shack they'd been living in before. Only now there were five of them. There was never a quiet moment in the house, and it seemed like the kids were always crying, whining, and fighting.

Mary, exhausted and overwhelmed, nagged Woody to get a job. He tried, but couldn't bear it. Besides, people in Pampa didn't exactly throw open their arms and welcome Woody back. They were angry he wouldn't settle down and work a regular job like other fathers. They whispered he was washed up as a musician and worse, he was a Commie. The small-town whispering that had hurt his family so badly in Okemah was going against Woody again. It didn't take long before he hit the road, this time alone.

On a freezing cold day in early January 1940, Woody grabbed his guitar and drove north during a Texas blizzard. Icy winds swept down on him at sixty miles an hour, making the car freeze up. He piled rags and an old sack on the engine and kept driving. Occasionally he'd stop to paint a sign in trade for gas, but his hands were so frozen he could barely hold the brush. He sold his spare tire, his car jack, and his brushes and kept heading north. Finally he even had to sell his guitar for three dollars.

When he had a little money in his pocket, Woody pulled into a roadside diner for a bowl of chili beans and a cup of coffee. Wherever he went, he heard a new song on the jukeboxes: "God Bless America." Trumpets and drums set a strong military cadence and violins soared to romantic heights as Kate Smith's lush voice extolled the virtues of her "home sweet home," America.

Kate Smith performing in a live radio broadcast with studio musicians.

"From the mountains to the prairies," she sang, "to the oceans white with foam." Written by Irving Berlin, the song romanticized America, telling people not to worry, that America was a wonderful place and everything would be all right. Woody didn't think everything was all right, with people starving in America and a catastrophic war in Europe.

By the time he pulled into Kowana, Oklahoma, Woody was "frozen stiff as a dead man." His engine quit and he coasted down a hill to Streetman's market, where his brother Roy was still working. Woody didn't stay long. He sold his broken-down car to Roy for thirty-five dollars, which gave him just enough money for a bus ticket as far as Pittsburgh, Pennsylvania.

As he made his way east he heard "God Bless America" over and over again. Snatches of words and different tunes swirled in Woody's thoughts as he scornfully played with the song in his mind.

Woody left the bus terminal in Pittsburgh and headed for the open road in another blizzard. There were no people or cars in sight. As he struggled over the bridge spanning the Susquehannah River, icy winds tore his hat off. Suddenly a forest ranger pulled up beside him in a car, and squeezed him into the back seat with a bunch of traps and cameras and animal skins.

The ranger took him home and filled him full of hot clam chowder. "I will never forget how good that hot clam juice tasted as it slid down my throat," Woody wrote later. "I had really given up all hopes of ever seeing any human beings alive on this planet any more, so this was really some big treat."

Woody showed up at Will and Herta's apartment in New York exhausted, filthy, and smelly. They were delighted to see him, but dismayed that he had no money and nowhere to go. They told him he could sleep on the couch, and Woody promptly took over the living room, staying up late, and sleeping until noon or later. Herta often stayed in the back bedroom with her new baby, not wanting to disturb Woody.

During the day, Woody jostled along the sidewalks with the seven million people living in New York City. After California and Texas, he found the people in New York City—more than a third of them foreign-born—fascinating. Woody squeezed onto the subways

The Bowery in New York City at Christmas time, 1942.

with Hassidic Jews with their black hats and side curls and Indian women in saris. He slipped into Orthodox churches, ate bagels and lox, and hung around Washington Square Park, listening to people perched on wooden boxes, haranguing passers by with their opinions on everything from Jesus to fascism.

Woody made a point of going down to the Bowery, New York's Skid Row. He was used to jumping off trains and heading for Skid Rows. For twenty cents he could sleep in a flophouse, and for only a few pennies get a cheap, filling bowl of beans. But what he saw in the Bowery shocked him. "Guys passed out drunk on the cement steps of the stores and banks," he wrote. "Draped around the light posts, slumped over the fire plugs, and sleeping around up against the bronze statues in the parks."

Usually comfortable on Skid Row, Woody was repelled. "I didn't know human beings could get so broke, hungry and so dirty and ragged and still remain alive. The wine they drink must come out through the pores of their skin and get the disease germs so drunk they can't organize."

Nights Woody went out to the bars, Herta's guitar slung over his shoulder. He'd spend hours talking to the other patrons in the bar, trading songs for a drink or two. In the early hours of the morning he'd head back to the apartment, often bringing new "friends" home with him. Herta and Will began dropping broad hints to Woody that he needed to find his own place.

Woody seemed oblivious. Nor could Herta and Will get through to him that he needed to bathe regularly. One evening Will was in the bath when Woody wandered in and sat on the closed toilet playing the guitar. Woody's hair was dirty and matted, and he smelled terrible. Will jumped out of the bath, grabbed Woody under the armpits, and swung him into the hot bathwater.

Herta's patience was running out. She spent lots of time crying in her room, feeling trapped by Woody sleeping on the couch, worrying that the baby might catch germs from him. Finally she wrote him a letter, telling him she loved him and wanted to help, but it was too hard living with him. As he lay sleeping one afternoon she put the letter on his chest then scurried back to the bedroom with the baby, feeling terribly guilty.

After hearing Woody wake up and open the letter, she went out to the living room. For a long moment they just looked at each other. Herta could see how hurt Woody was. Without a word he picked up her guitar and walked out the door.

Woody and folk singer Burl Ives in Central Park, New York, 1940.

Chapter Six
1940-1941
Hitting the Big Time

"With all these poor folks wandering around the country as homeless as little doggies, what I should do is strap on a couple of six-shooters and blow open the doors of the bank and feed people and give them houses. The only reason I don't do that is because I ain't got the guts."

Woody found a room at the Hanover House, a cheap, fleabag hotel near Times Square. At a critical juncture in his life, Woody was full of impassioned ideas about what was wrong with the country and how to fix it. He knew how to write and sing songs he was sure would help, but he wasn't connected yet with people who could get his message out.

Alone and frustrated, he fought his way out the only way he knew: by writing another of his hard-bitten songs about how life really was. This time he took on Irving Berlin's "God Bless America."

Sitting in his rundown hotel room, Woody pulled out a piece of lined paper and wrote across the top of the page, "God Blessed America." One by one he wrote down the verses that had been forming in his mind, until he had six in all. He wrote about what he saw as he rambled: rolling dust clouds, hungry people waiting in relief lines, private property signs. And with a tender simplicity, he wrote of the splendor and joy of being out on the road, walking across America's golden valleys and diamond deserts. In his even, clear writing, he added at the bottom, "All you can write is what you see," and signed it "Woody G., Feb. 23, 1940."

As he sat staring out the window of his room, Woody's mercurial mind jumped to the streets of New York City.

> I saw how the poor folks lived, and then I saw how the rich folks lived, and the poor folks down and out and cold and hungry, and the rich ones out drinking good whiskey and celebrating and wasting handfuls of money at gambling and women, and I got to thinking about what Jesus said, and what if He was to walk into New York City and preach like He use to. They'd lock Him back in jail as sure as you're reading this.

In those bleak, cold winter months he wrote several versions of his song "Jesus Christ," then a second song, "A Hard Working Man Is Jesus." Though angered by the "meek shall inherit the earth" aspect of Christianity, Woody embraced Jesus as a man working outside the system, dedicated to the needs of the poor. For a few weeks, his mind returned again and again to Jesus. "It ain't just once in awhile that I think about this man, it's mighty scarce that I think of anything else," he wrote.

While Woody was rambling the streets, writing songs and staving off the loneliness he felt at night, Will Geer had been busy putting together a *Grapes of Wrath* benefit concert. Based on Steinbeck's novel, the movie had just opened at the Rivoli Theater in New York City. Appalled by life in the California fields, people wanted to help. Will asked a group of leading folksingers to appear in the show and made sure Woody, an authentic Okie, would be there.

On March 3, 1940, Aunt Molly Jackson led off the evening at the Forrest Theater. The wife of a leading coal striker, she'd been organizing the miners and writing songs about the

Original version of "This Land Is Your Land," 1940. Woody first titled his song "God Blessed America," then renamed it "This Land Was Made for You and Me." Finally it became known as "This Land Is Your Land."

God Blessed America
This Land Was made For You & me

This land is your land, this land is my land
From California to the New York Island,
From the Redwood Forest, to the Gulf stream waters,
God blessed America for me.

As I went walking that ribbon of highway
And saw above me that endless skyway,
And saw below me the golden valley, I said:
God blessed America for me.

I roamed and rambled, and followed my footsteps
To the sparkling sands of her diamond deserts,
And all around me, a voice was sounding:
God blessed America for me.

Was a big high wall there that tried to stop me
A sign was painted said: Private Property.
But on the back side it didn't say nothing —
God blessed America for me.

When the sun come shining, then I was strolling
In wheat fields waving, and dust clouds rolling;
The voice was chanting as the fog was lifting:
God blessed America for me.

One bright sunny morning in the shadow of the steeple
By the Relief office I saw my people —
As they stood hungry, I stood there wondering if
God blessed America for me.

* all you can write is
what you see.

original copy
of this song

Woody G.
N.Y., N.Y., N.Y.
Feb. 23, 1940
43rd st & 6th Ave,
Hanover House

abysmal conditions of the Kentucky mines until death threats forced her to relocate to New York City.

Woody milled around in the wings as she sang, the heat from the lights bringing out the musty smell of the theater. When Aunt Molly finished he ambled out, wearing a cowboy hat, boots, and blue jeans. After scratching his head with his guitar pick, he greeted the crowd with a simple "Howdy" and stood looking into the darkened theater. Finally he launched into a song, then he was going—singing his Dust Bowl songs in a flat Oklahoma twang and spinning out stories.

Standing in the wings, Alan Lomax was galvanized by Woody. Only twenty-four years old, he was already the Acting Director for the Archive of Folk Song at the Library of Congress in Washington. He and his father, John Lomax, had been crossing and recrossing the United States, recording folk music they thought would soon be lost forever.

Alan Lomax was afraid that folk music, the *real* music of America, was a dying tradition, with popular songs constantly blaring from radio stations across America. When he heard Woody singing, he knew instantly he was listening to someone who understood the power and strength of folk songs, yet knew how to adapt them into political songs. The songs Woody wrote were brilliant, easy to learn and remember. Lomax was sure he was listening to a genius. He could barely wait for the concert to end so he could talk with Woody.

One of the last performers was a tall, gawky young man named Pete Seeger, who came onto the stage with a five-string banjo and launched into the "Ballad of John Hardy." It was late, the audience was tired, and this was Pete's very first appearance. He rushed his playing until his fingers jumbled and froze up, his mind went blank, and he couldn't remember the words. The audience clapped politely at his attempt, and Pete fled the stage.

Later many people, including Alan Lomax, felt the *Grapes of Wrath* concert was the spark that popularized folk music in America. The songs were haunting, joyful, tragic, and revealing; the singers passionate, determined to create social change. The lineup that night seemed to cover just about everything, from ballads about the bloody miners struggle in

Kentucky to the powerful prison work songs of the Deep South.

As soon as he was able to talk with Woody after the concert, Lomax wasted no time telling him what he wanted: When could Woody get down to Washington, D.C., to be recorded? How many songs did he know, anyway?

Nothing was holding Woody in New York, and in about a week he was in Washington, staying with Lomax and his wife. He turned down their offer of a bed, and fell asleep

Concert at the Forrest Theater in New York City, 1940. Alan Lomax is on the left, and Woody is squatting in front with his guitar.

sprawled on the couch, or threw his lumber jacket over his shoulders and slept on the floor. Rather than eat at the table, he insisted on standing over the sink, saying, "I don't want to get softened up. I'm a road man." Pete Seeger, working at the archive with Lomax for fifteen dollars a week, turned up frequently, eager to learn anything he could from this singing "road man."

Lomax was amazed when he brought Woody to the recording studio on March 21, 1940. Woody knew hundreds of folk songs—traditional, gospel, cowboy, country, and mountain songs he had picked up in Oklahoma, Texas, and California. Then there were

Woody with banjo player Lilly Mae Ledford and Alan Lomax, early 1940s.

dozens more songs he had adapted to his politics, modifying tunes and putting new words to folk songs he knew. Between singing his songs, he talked about his life and philosophies with Lomax.

Woody explained how he saw the blues.

> I've always called it being lonesome. You can get lonesome for a lot of things. You can get lonesome for a job, lonesome for some spending money, lonesome for some drinking whiskey, lonesome for a good time, pretty gals, wine women and song. Thinking that you are down and out and disgusted and busted and can't be trusted, why, it gives you a lonesome feeling. Somehow the world has sorta turned against you.

Woody was also painfully honest when Lomax asked him if he'd gone through any hard times in Oklahoma. "I never did talk it much," Woody said, but then he went on, almost as if he couldn't stop himself, to describe his sister Clara's fiery death. He claimed Clara either set herself on fire, or caught fire accidentally. "There's two different stories got out about it," Woody said. "She had to stay home and do some work and she caught afire while she was doing some ironing that afternoon on the old kerosene stove. She run around the house about twice before anybody could catch her, and the next day she died." Woody cleared his throat, the microphone amplifying the sound.

"And my mother . . . that was a little bit too much for her nerves or something . . . I don't know exactly how it was, but anyway, my mother died in the insane asylum at Norman, Oklahoma."

Woody was silent for a long moment, then spoke again. "My father, mysteriously for some reason, caught fire. All us kids had to scatter out."

Suddenly Woody veered off, leaving the vulnerable, painful parts of his childhood behind. He launched into a funny story and didn't reveal anything so personal to Lomax again.

His recording done, Woody returned to New York. He hadn't been back long when a record producer approached him about writing a song based on *The Grapes of Wrath.* Woody asked Pete Seeger, in town visiting a friend, if he had a typewriter so he could work on the song.

"Have you read the book?" Pete asked him.

"Nope," Woody responded, "but I saw the movie—good movie."

There was a typewriter where Pete was staying, so he invited Woody over, who brought a half-gallon jug of cheap wine. For the next hour, Pete watched Woody type a line or two, stand up and pluck out something on his guitar, then sit back down to work out a few more lines. Around ten Pete finally fell asleep. When he woke up in the morning the jug was empty, Woody was asleep under the table, and the finished song was in the typewriter. Written to the tune of "John Hardy," Woody's seventeen-verse song "Tom Joad" summarized the entire story.

Woody on the lawn at Highlander Folk School, 1940.

Woody considered his song one of the best he'd ever done. Late in April 1940, at Lomax's urging, Victor Records recorded an album of Woody singing "Tom Joad," "Dust Bowl Refugee," "I Ain't Got No Home," "Do Re Mi," "So Long It's Been Good to Know Yuh," and eight of his other Dust Bowl songs. Woody was ecstatic—and shocked—when he was paid three hundred dollars for his day's work.

For the first time in his life, Woody put a down payment on a new car. He talked Pete Seeger into coming with him, and headed out to visit Mary and the kids in Texas.

They made an odd pair. Pete was tall, lanky, and extremely naive, from an upper-class New England family. Woody couldn't understand Pete. "I can't make him out," he told a friend. "He doesn't look at girls, he doesn't drink, he doesn't smoke, the fellow's weird."

Always glad to be back on the road, Woody was thrilled to be driving a brand-new car. Finally, he didn't have to worry about engine trouble—nothing to seize up or break down. In fact the car was so powerful he bragged to Lomax, "In the Blue Ridge Mountains me and Pete almost got it to climb a tree."

Woody and Pete Seeger playing at the Highlander Folk School, 1940.

Woody sent a constant stream of letters from the road to family and friends. He signed off, "Take it easy, but take it," a habit he would continue for years.

Despite driving a brand-new car, Woody still liked to travel as cheaply as possible. As they drove west, he taught Pete how to get free drinks in a bar: Take your banjo out of the case, go inside, and order a nickel beer.

"Sooner or later somebody's gonna say, 'Kid can you pick that thing?'" Woody explained. "Don't be in too big a hurry, just keep on sippin' your beer. Sooner or later somebody's gonna say, 'Kid, I got a quarter for you, if you pick us a tune.' Now you swing it around and play your best tune."

They drove through Tennessee and stopped at the Highlander Folk School, a training center for labor organizers. Then they sped west, rolling across Arkansas and into Oklahoma, where they saw Roy, Mary Jo, and Charley Guthrie. They only stayed a few hours, though. Pete felt a painful tension between Woody and his father.

In Oklahoma City they dropped in on Bob and Ina Wood, local Communist party organizers, who immediately sent them down to the local migrant camp by the Canadian River to entertain the desperate, down-and-out families. That evening, Ina, an ardent feminist, lectured Woody for never writing any songs about the hard work and courage of women in the labor movement.

Before going to bed, Woody borrowed her typewriter and turned out a crisp, beautiful song, "Union Maid." The song gradually became widely known, and was sung on picket lines and in union halls across the country.

> There once was a union maid
> who never was afraid
> of goons and ginks and company finks
> and the deputy sheriffs who made the raid.
>
> She went to the union hall
> when a meeting it was called,
> And when the company boys came 'round
> she always stood her ground.
>
> Oh, you can't scare me,
> I'm sticking to the union.
> I'm sticking to the union,
> Till the day I die.

Police using tear gas against striking workers at the Newton Steel Company in Monroe, Michigan, 1937. The women are fighting back.

Finally they arrived in Pampa. Pete was struck by how shy Mary was, and desperate. She had the weary, worn-out look of a young mother with too much responsibility and not enough help. And Woody's erratic behavior had forced her to fall back on her parents for support, a difficult situation for everyone. "Is that the price of genius?" Pete asked himself. "Is it worth paying?"

But his allegiances were split. Years later he said, "Lord, Lord, he turned out song after song!"

When Pete met Mary's mother, she grabbed him by the shoulders and shook him. "You've got to get that man to start treating my daughter right!" But nobody could make Woody do what he didn't want to do. A few days later, Pete and Woody took off.

Back in New York, Woody kept bumming from place to place. One of the other singers from the *Grapes of Wrath* concert, Leadbelly, let Woody sleep on the Murphy bed, which folded out of the wall in the living room. Leadbelly would get up early, and his wife, Martha, insisted Woody get up, shave, and wash while she made breakfast.

Already in his early fifties, Leadbelly was a burly, tender man with a deep sense of pride. Jailed twice, each time for killing a man in a barroom fight, he'd spent years in the repressive prisons of the Deep South. Woody loved being around Leadbelly, soaking up musical lore from him.

In concerts, Leadbelly sang full out, his deep voice booming over the crowd, while he expertly picked the guitar, jumping up from time to time to tap-dance or do the "buck and wing." Known for his haunting renditions of blues and work songs, Leadbelly sometimes explained the blues to his audience.

> The blues is like this. You lay down some night and you turn from one side of the bed to the other, all night long. It's not too cold in that bed, and it ain't too hot. But what's the matter? The blues has got you and they want to talk with you.

Woody playing with Leadbelly in Chicago, 1941. *Courtesy of the Chicago Historical Society*

Woody especially loved Leadbelly's gentle side. Mornings in the quiet apartment, Leadbelly played at about half-speed, gently picking quiet tunes on his twelve-string guitar.

> He had a slow running, easy, deep quiet way about him, that
> made me see that his strength was like a little ball in his hands,
> and that his thoughts ran as deep in color as the lights that
> played down from the sky and onto his face.

In August , Woody signed a contract for $150 a week to be on a radio show called *Back*

Where I Come From. At the same time he met up with Cisco Houston, who'd sung with him and Will Geer in the California migrant camps. Cisco found a job as a doorman in a burlesque house on Forty-second Street and decided to stick around New York for a while.

Tall and handsome, Cisco was a generous man with a warm, lonely tenor voice, which harmonized beautifully with Woody's. Delighted to see him, Woody quickly persuaded Cisco to join him singing in clubs and bars. Like Matt Jennings back in Pampa, Cisco loved music, didn't talk much, and was awed by Woody's freewheeling, wild life. Cisco would prove to be one of Woody's closest friends.

Shortly after Cisco showed up, the Model Tobacco Company signed Woody on as the host of another radio show for two hundred dollars a week. Woody was overwhelmed by the sudden attention and huge sums of money being thrust at him. "They are giving me money so fast I'm using it to sleep under," he wrote Lomax. He sent Mary and the kids the unbelievable sum of three hundred dollars.

But all the money being offered Woody raised serious questions for him. What was he, a poor Okie, doing taking in so much money when people everywhere were hungry? Was he selling out?

And once again his politics surfaced as a problem. Was he or wasn't he a Communist party member? Big companies like Model Tobacco couldn't afford to have Communists on their shows—they'd lose all their sponsors. Woody wrote a nervous, defensive letter to Lomax.

> They called me a communist and a wild man and everything
> you could think of but I don't care what they call me. I aint a
> member of any earthy organization my trouble is I really ought
> to go down there in the morning and just join everything.

The Model Tobacco company believed him, and when the show aired in November 1940, Woody rented an apartment and sent for Mary and the kids. Mary bundled the kids

Promotional flyer from the Model Tobacco Company radio show, 1940.

onto a train, arriving three days later in Grand Central Station. Woody was nowhere to be seen, and Mary was petrified by the enormous, crowded station. She dragged the kids around the station in a panic looking for Woody before piling them into a taxi, giving the driver the address Woody had sent her. Finally Woody showed up at the apartment, delighted to see them, and drove them all to the Bronx Zoo in his new car.

Mary and the kids settled quickly into the apartment. It was the nicest place they'd ever lived in. For the first time in their lives together, Woody and Mary had plenty of money. They could hire a sitter to watch the kids and go out at night. It was almost too much for Mary to believe. She had been right all along, Woody was making it big. All those whispering neighbors in Pampa were wrong. Woody was being recorded, and playing and singing on the radio. Who knew what was ahead?

To his dismay, Woody found the Model Tobacco show was tightly scripted. The producers insisted Woody sing only his mildest songs. When he narrated, he wasn't allowed to make wisecrack political asides—everything had to be read off the script. For a couple of weeks Woody swallowed his pride and did as he was told, but he found it humiliating to follow other people's directions. Without the sly political jabs, and his caustic, hard-hitting songs, he was just another country hick, lost and overwhelmed by the big city. As the weeks went by, his mood worsened. He found everything frustrating, even having his family with him. He wrote a takeoff on one of his own songs, "It Takes a Married Man to Sing a Worried Song."

By the time the holidays came, Mary could feel something in Woody hitting the explosion point. Cisco dropped by on Christmas Eve, and to his deep embarrassment, Woody talked him into going out to a nearby bar. It was early Christmas morning before they returned.

On New Year's Eve Woody played at a fancy fund-raiser Will Geer had set up. The women were dressed in full-length evening gowns and the men in white shirts and tuxedos. The room was packed with wealthy, important people. Woody sang three or four songs, very badly, with his eyes shut. Will slipped over to him and asked him why his eyes were closed.

"All them white shirts and diamonds are blinding me," said Woody.

Will, furious with Woody, whispered to him that these were some of the most important people in New York.

"They act like it," Woody replied.

A few days later, Woody suddenly announced to Mary they were leaving town. Mary was frustrated and upset. Woody was throwing everything away—again. She figured there must be something in him that rejected steadiness, or success. Something. It sure didn't make any sense.

That evening she and Woody ran up and down the stairs to their apartment, cramming what they could into the car, leaving everything else. In the middle of the night they pulled out of town.

It was a strange, frightening trip. They ran into a terrible wind and rain storm in Washington, where Sue said she wanted to go home and asked her mother where home was. Mary didn't know what to say. By this time she had no idea, and she was pretty sure Woody didn't either.

Their crazy, wild rush across America took them all the way to a dilapidated hotel in Columbia, California, an old ghost town in the Sierra foothills. Woody was restless and agitated. He didn't want to be in New York, but he wasn't happy in a tiny, deserted town either. After a few weeks he told Mary they were moving again, this time back to Los Angeles.

Chapter Seven
1941-1942

On the Road Again

"I have always been hot-tempered and stubborn and full of lots of nervous energy, and in my banging around over the country, I found my only fuel was to be very independent, stand alone, contrive, invent, imagine, and as time rolled along, I got a smattering of political education."

They arrived at Ed Robbins's house in Los Angeles late one rainy night, exhausted and cold. Ed and his wife welcomed them, fed them a hot meal, and pulled out blankets and mattresses. The house was tiny, with only one small bedroom for Ed, his wife and two kids. For the next few days bedding was laid wall-to-wall for everybody to sleep.

Ed mentioned to Woody that the house next door was vacant, ever since the owner, Mrs. Wolfson, had moved to nearby Pasadena. Ed thought they ought to drive out to Pasadena and see if the house was available to rent.

"You mean it's empty?" said Woody.

"She's been out of there a couple of months," Ed replied.

"Well, let's get going."

Ed thought Woody meant get going to Pasadena to see the owner, but a few minutes later Woody had pried open a window and moved Mary and the kids into the house. Ed and Woody drove around visiting Ed's friends, collecting furniture and kitchen tools, and soon the house was set up.

Woody in his Los Angeles back yard, 1941.

Woody with Mary and their children, Teeny, Sue, and Billy, in Los Angeles, 1941.

Woody dropped in at KFVD to see if he could get his old job back, but Frank Burke wanted nothing to do with him. Though he couldn't get a radio program going, Woody was welcomed at the camps, where life was still difficult and pleasure in short supply. Even though his audiences weren't big, they were deeply appreciative, finding him inspiring—an Okie singing about the poor and downtrodden—and larger than life. Woody wrote Pete Seeger, "On more than one night, on more than one day, I've heard my Okie friends ask me, Say, mister, you dont happen to be Mister Jesus do you? Come back?"

A left-wing writer who knew Woody from his radio station days, Jack Weatherwax, decided to put together a fund-raising party for the migrants. He asked Woody to be the main attraction. Woody was delighted, and a few weeks before the event they drove down to Arvin camp with Jack's wife, Seema, a photographer, to invite the migrant families to come to the party.

They set out early in the morning, the air clean and crisp after a night rain. Woody drove full-throttle, throwing his head back and singing the entire way down to the camp, never repeating himself, coming up with new songs and verses as they drove along.

Woody talking with Fred Ross, manager of the Shafter Farm Workers Community, 1941. John Steinbeck used Shafter camp as the background for some of the Joad family's struggles in *The Grapes of Wrath*.

Seema Weatherwax was amazed by the car: an enormous, shiny black Buick. Woody told her how he'd chosen it back in New York. He'd strolled into a dealership, flush with all the money he was making. "I want the longest car you have," he said, and ended up with a luxury Buick. But months of travel had trashed the car—the upholstery was torn and stained, the fenders dented and windows broken. Woody was having trouble making the payments to keep the car, but he didn't seem worried.

When they arrived at the camp, Woody unslung his guitar and started to sing. As the crowd grew around him, Seema wandered off, camera in hand, photographing. She found hot showers, day care for the kids while the parents worked in the fields, classes, and work crews.

A few weeks later the fund-raising party drew a crowd of over two hundred people. A band played, and people joined hands to dance and talk and laugh in big circles. Kids ran around stuffing themselves from the food tables. All kinds of contests were held, including one to see which kid had the most freckles. The party was a big hit except for one missing element: Woody.

Jack Weatherwax nervously took the stage and started telling long, involved stories, not sure if he was trying to hold the crowd for Woody or wrap things up. Just before eleven, Woody strolled in, walked casually onto the stage, and started playing.

With performances few and far between, Woody poured his creative energy into writing. He began work on an autobiographic novel, his sentences long, wild, and uncensored. He was often at home, pounding away on the typewriter, the kids crawling all over him as he worked. But with so few outlets for his music, Woody was having a hard time. "Today is lonesome and sad as the devil," he wrote. "Everything looks like it's all bogged down. But we'll pull through. Always do."

But the feelings boiling up inside him were tense and unpredictable. One night he got blind, staggering drunk and stood outside the house, hurling beer bottles through the windows. Mary grabbed the kids and ran next door to Ed's until his rage burned itself out.

Men and children cluster around Woody as he gives an impromptu concert at Shafter camp, 1941. The photographer noticed few women. She found them in their tents, doing chores and caring for the babies and toddlers.

While they were in Los Angeles, Woody insisted on dragging Mary to classes on Communism at the Workers' School, which she found threatening. Though she knew it was useless to argue with him, she could no longer quietly accept his view of the world, and she and Woody started having loud, screaming fights.

Woody couldn't believe Mary stuck to her Catholicism. He was angry that she "hated all of my new books and new friends and my new found thoughts with a poison in her belly that killed everything I tried to learn." The worst part was their children overhearing their "mean, despiteful and hateful kinds of arguments."

In May, Woody heard a documentary film was going to be made in Portland, Oregon. The Bonneville Power Administration wanted to show the benefits of the new dam they were building across the Columbia River. Building the dam created jobs, and once the power of the river was harnessed, the government could provide cheap electricity for all the small, hardscrabble farms.

Once again, Woody piled Mary and the kids into the car, and they headed for Portland. It was a hard, fast trip. The money from New York was long gone, and at one point Woody was forced to pull out the car radio and trade it for food.

Woody walked into the Bonneville Power Administration office rumpled, unwashed, and unshaven. The head of the project felt both sympathetic and intrigued. What could this road-weary Okie pull off? After an hour of listening to Woody sing and play the guitar, the project head gave him a month's pay of $266.66 and asked him to write the songs for the movie.

For the next month, Woody traipsed up and down the Columbia River, thrilled that the government was building this huge dam. He loved watching the burly, sweating construction workers working—pouring concrete, driving tractors and bulldozers, moving huge amounts of dirt. He rambled around, asking questions, watching, listening, and daydreaming, all the while scribbling madly in a small notebook.

A view of the construction work on the Bonneville Dam, May 1936. The excavations are more than sixty feet below the surface of the river.

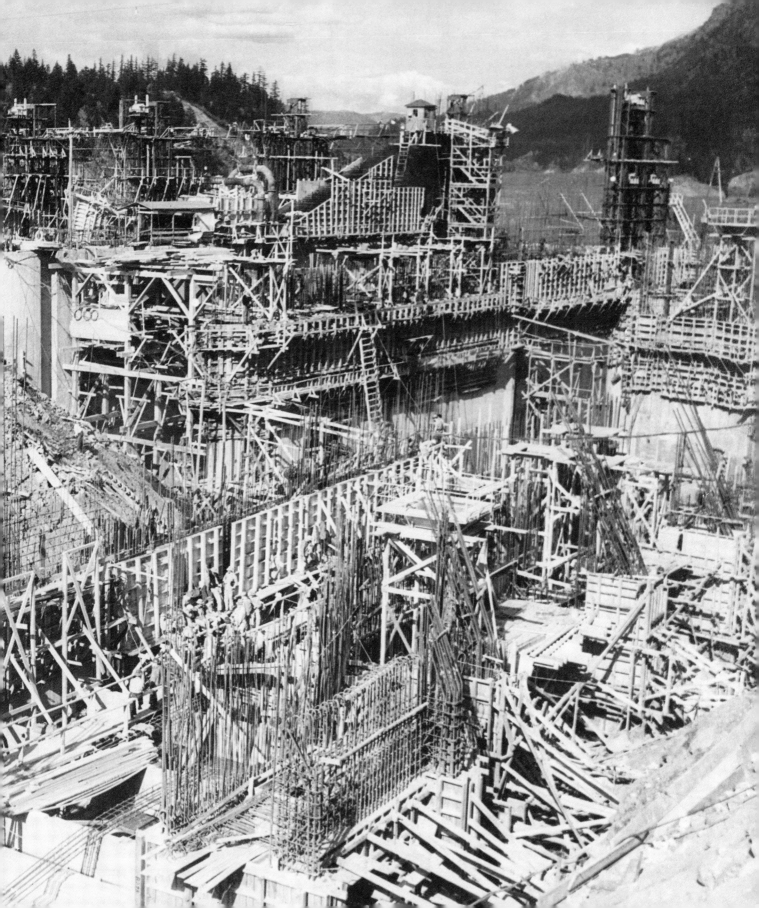

It was an incredibly prolific period for Woody. Songs like "Roll On, Columbia" tumbled out of him as if the river were running right through him, filling him with excitement. Typing furiously at night, he finished twenty-six songs by the end of the month. In an inspired sweep of lyrics, he wrote "Pastures of Plenty," celebrating the river, the fertile land it nourished, and America's need to be free from the fascism taking over Europe.

> Well it's always we ramble this river and I,
> All along your green valleys I'll work till I die,
> My land I'll defend with my life if it be,
> 'Cause my pastures of plenty must always be free.

And then it was all over. The songs were finished, the paycheck was spent, and there was no further need for him. The car company caught up with Woody and repossessed the car. From elation, Woody fell back to the bottom, ready to start scrounging again, wondering which way to turn, where to go. He was saved by a letter from Pete Seeger and two men he was singing with. They were arranging a summer tour and wanted to know if he could join them.

That was all the encouragement Woody needed, and he took off, leaving Mary and the kids behind in Portland, where they didn't know anyone.

But Woody wasn't thinking about Mary. He was rattling east in a freight train, looking forward to being on the road, playing music, and talking politics.

While Woody was trying to make a life for himself on the West Coast, Pete Seeger had returned to New York, full of fervor and a passionate desire to make a difference with his banjo and his singing. He was determined to use folk music to organize workers and strengthen the growing union movement. He teamed up with another left-wing musician, Lee Hays.

An enormous, burly twenty-seven-year-old, Lee had a staggering array of health

Lee Hays, at a hootenanny at the Old Town School of Folk Music, Chicago.

problems, drank and ate way more than he should, and complained constantly. But when it came to singing, he had a rumbling bass voice that rolled out of him with a Baptist fervor. Brilliant and uncompromising, he knew how to make a few simple word changes and turn any church song into an effective union song.

Lee liked the percussive, vibrant sound of Pete's banjo, and Pete admired Lee's easy, comfortable way with an audience. They began singing for left-wing causes all around New York City. Soon they brought in Millard Lampell, a writer from New Jersey, who amazed them by making up sharp, sassy verses in just minutes. In Madison Square Garden they sang for twenty thousand striking transport workers, and soon unions all over the east coast wanted them to perform.

The Almanacs, as they named themselves, came up with dozens of union songs. They also wrote and sang peace songs, urging America to stay out of the "European War." Their songs were "full of guts and just as poignant as hell," Lee said.

But on June 22, 1941, as Woody was rolling east, Hitler's armies smashed into the Soviet Union, shattering the nonaggression pact and ending the neutrality favored by many American Communists.

A few days later Woody arrived in New York, and knocked on the door of the Almanacs' house. When Pete opened the door, Woody grinned at him and said, "Well, I guess we won't be singing any more peace songs, will we?" Pete and the other Almanacs had been fiercely debating the issue, and had come to the same conclusion. It was clear that Hitler would only be stopped by force. Peace songs were out.

"Our whole politics took a terrible shift from 'the Yanks ain't coming' to 'the Yanks ARE coming,'" said Lee. "But it sure knocked hell out of our repertoire." Suddenly they had only union songs to fall back on, and they started quickly making up new songs.

Gathering in the living room, they took turns tossing out ideas, bickering, shouting out lyrics and trying out new melodies. Woody was the acknowledged leader. With his guitar cradled in his lap, he'd fire off songs, bully the others, and shoot down ideas he thought were too heavy-handed or commercial. The others let him take the lead. After all, he was the authentic Okie, with more writing and performing experience than all the rest of them rolled together. But they reined him in, changing lyrics, suggesting tunes, fighting to make the songs strong. Together they achieved a magical synthesis, and the songs rolled out, glorious, timely, easy to sing and remember.

In early July the Almanacs headed out in an old gas-guzzling limousine that Millard had bought for $125 from a dead gangster's family. They'd find their way to a union hall, pile out of the car, and grab their instruments. They sang before and after the speakers, and then took up a collection of money for gas, oil, and food. They used everything in their repertoire, including "Union Maid," "Talking Union," "I Don't Want Your Millions Mister," "Get Thee Behind Me Satan," and "Union Train." And as they drove along or stayed with friendly workers, they made up more songs, working their way through Philadelphia, Pittsburgh, Cleveland, Chicago, Milwaukee, finally arriving in San Francisco in early August. They had plenty of interested audiences: There were nearly 2.5 million workers on strike across America.

The Almanacs didn't know it, but they were being followed. The Federal Bureau of Investigation was keeping secret files on all people and groups they thought were subversive. An undercover FBI informant reported the Almanacs were "extremely untidy, ragged and dirty in appearance." The rousing song-leading technique of the group didn't fool the informant for one second. "After going through the song once, the majority of the audience joined in the singing," he wrote. "They joined in not from their own desire, but were led into it through mass psychology and apathy toward the utter control of the meeting by Communist officers and members."

The Almanac Singers in 1941. From left: Woody, Millard Lampell, Bess Lomax, Pete Seeger, Arthur Stern, and Sis Cunningham.

The Almanacs wrapped up their trip with a rousing, successful appearance before the dock workers in San Francisco. Lee didn't feel well and took the train back to New York, but Pete, Millard, and Woody went on to Los Angeles, where they spent the rest of August playing for picket lines, parties, and meetings.

While they were in Los Angeles, Mary and the kids arrived from Portland. Woody was distant and uncaring, Mary desperate. In a month Teeny would be starting school. It was time to settle down. Where was Woody planning to be? Woody offered to take them back to New York, but warned Mary he would be out on the road most of the time. The offer didn't interest Mary. She gathered up the kids and took the train back to Pampa. It was a sad, painful ending for both of them.

"Neither one of us could take each other's presence anymore," Woody said, "and we just closed up our ears and eyes and minds toward each other, till she moved back to Texas."

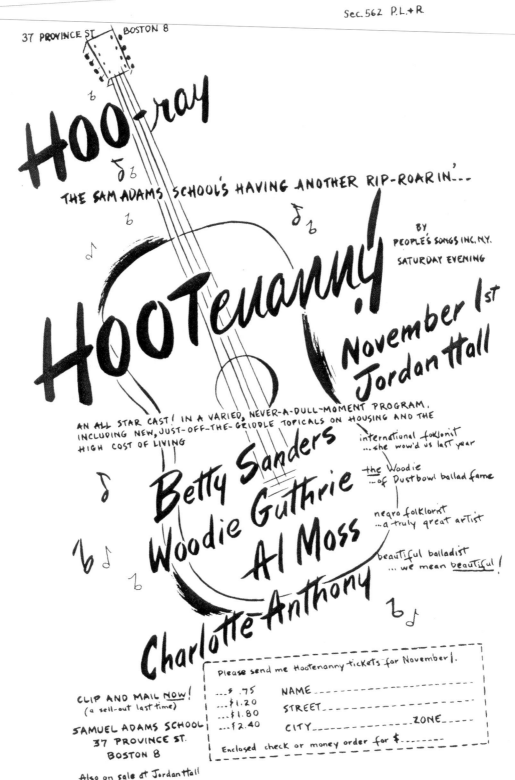

37 PROVINCE ST   BOSTON 8

HOO-ray

THE SAM ADAMS SCHOOL'S HAVING ANOTHER RIP-ROARIN'...

BY
PEOPLE'S SONGS INC. N.Y.
SATURDAY EVENING

Hootenanny!

November 1st
Jordan Hall

AN ALL STAR CAST! IN A VARIED, NEVER-A-DULL-MOMENT PROGRAM,
INCLUDING NEW, JUST-OFF-THE-GRIDDLE TOPICALS ON HOUSING AND THE
HIGH COST OF LIVING

Betty Sanders   international folklorist
...she wow'd us last year

Woodie Guthrie   the Woodie
...of Dustbowl ballad fame

Al Moss   negro folklorist
...a truly great artist

Charlotte Anthony   beautiful balladist
... we mean beautiful!

CLIP AND MAIL NOW!
(a sell-out last time)

SAMUEL ADAMS SCHOOL
37 PROVINCE ST.
BOSTON 8

Also on sale at Jordan Hall

Please send me Hootenanny tickets for November 1.

...$ .75   NAME_____
...$1.20   STREET_____
...$1.80   CITY_____ZONE_____
...$2.40

Enclosed check or money order for $_____

Mary was no happier about it. "You want to know how I felt?" she confided later to a friend. "I felt rotten. It was bitter. I was hardly part of his life and that was why I finally decided to get out of it all and I left and went back home. I couldn't see any future for us in all this."

Millard headed back to New York, and Pete and Woody drove north, singing their way through Portland, Seattle, and Minneapolis. They were eager to get back to New York City and rejoin Millard and Lee.

The Almanacs found a large house at Tenth Street and Sixth Avenue for ninety-five dollars a month and were joined by several others: Sis Cunningham and her husband, Gordon Friesen; Arthur Stern; and Bess Lomax, Alan Lomax's sister. To pay the rent they held Sunday afternoon gatherings called "hootenannies." People paid a small amount to squeeze into the basement and play music. Lee baked bread, the Almanacs bought a couple of jugs of cheap wine, and everyone sang and argued until their voices were hoarse and the wine and bread were long gone.

Pete tried to keep order in the house, but the place was a chaotic mess, even though cooking, cleaning, and household chores were supposed to be shared equally. The house was cluttered with song sheets, dirty cups and plates, musical instruments, and tossed-off clothing. A cleaning woman came once and refused to come back.

Flier advertising a Hootenanny (opposite page). Woody's explanation of a "hootenanny" appeared in *Time* magazine (right).

Hootenanny

"We was playin' for the Lumber Worker's Union. We was singin' around in the shingle mills. There was a lady out West there in the lumber camp and her name was Annie and so every time they'd have a songfest Annie would out shout all of them. So people got to call her Hootin' Annie but the name got spread all over and so out there when they are going to have a shindig they call it a "Hootenanny."

And that's how Hootenannies began, according to Woodrow Wilson ("Woody") Guthrie. Last week one of the shoutin'est Hootenannies ever was held in Irving Plaza's second floor dance hall a block from Manhattan's Union Square. On stage were 20 folk singers with guitars, mandolins and harmonicas. In the audience were 1,000 men, women & children (some also with guitars) who sang along with them. Smallest and loudest of them all was curly-haired Woody Guthrie. He sang:

Down in the henhouse, on my knees,
I thought I heard a chicken sneeze,
It was only a rooster, saying his prayers,
And giving out thanks to the hens
upstairs.

Time, April 15, 1946

Leadbelly and other musicians came by on Sundays to play music, often staying until the early hours of the morning. Josh White, son of a southern preacher, came by with his guitar, and Mother Bloor, a powerful speaker and organizer for the Communist party, dropped by to talk and listen to music, bringing apples from her orchard.

Bess Lomax, the only Almanac with an outside job, rose early while everyone else slept off the previous night's talking, singing, and drinking. She often found Woody asleep in the living room, draped over the typewriter, an empty wine bottle beside him, typed pages scattered all over the floor.

Whenever and wherever they could, the Almanacs played: meetings, parties, bars, even the subway. They usually charged ten dollars to sing and made fifty or sixty a week. All the money they earned was dropped into a communal kitty. When people called to book them, the Almanacs wouldn't guarantee who would appear. Whoever was around went to the booking—usually two to five people, but sometimes more. And they weren't always in top form. Woody said they were the only group that rehearsed onstage.

Money was tight, and people fought about who took money out of the kitty and what they spent it on. Woody threw money in the pot along with the others, but felt perfectly justified in taking out money for wine and cigarettes. Pete thought the money should be spent on more important things, like food and the utility bills that they were having trouble paying.

Whenever there was enough money in the kitty, Woody sent some to Mary. Now that his anger had cooled off, he was more sympathetic to her position. "I think thousands of young people make the same mistake my wife and I made, mainly, we married very young, we found ourselves drifting in opposite ways and as time went on I just had to leave and do her the justice of letting her discover a new life with a person more companionable."

In the fall, at Alan Lomax's urging, the Almanacs invited two musicians from the South to come to New York, sending them money for bus tickets. A few weeks later, Brownie McGhee, a blues singer and guitarist, and Sonny Terry, a blind harmonica player from Georgia, moved into the Almanac house. Brownie, struck with polio when he was four or five, walked with a limp, dragging one leg forward.

Sonny Terry (left) and Brownie McGhee. This photo was used in a newspaper advertisement for the first Folkways concert at Town Hall in New York City, 1946, where they appeared with Leadbelly.

Brownie and Sonny both loved to perform, but Brownie couldn't walk carrying his suitcase and guitar, and Sonny couldn't see to get around. Brownie explained how they'd come up with a solution: "Our deal was that he'd carry my weight and I'd see for him."

Woody and the other Almanacs were determined to promote integration by singing and living with black musicians. But they couldn't change society all at once, and black and white musicians were treated differently. Sometimes Sonny and Brownie were told to leave by the back door after a performance. Sometimes "they were playing our music on juke-boxes and we weren't allowed in the places!" Sonny said.

Sonny and Brownie loved the music and the activity, but were most comfortable when Leadbelly came by. It wasn't long before Leadbelly said to them, "I know that you guys ain't getting enough to eat there, you can't eat no pumpernickel bread. You ain't used to it." He invited them to come and live with him and Martha.

Brownie and Sonny began sleeping on the Murphy bed that Woody had been using the year before. Leadbelly asked Brownie, "If a white man calls you a nigger, what would you do?" Brownie replied, "I'd leave it to his ignorance, I wouldn't say anything. My daddy taught me don't let words hurt you. Grievous words stir up anger, so try to stay out of the way." Brownie and Sonny were much younger than Leadbelly, but the three of them became good friends.

As the cold of winter gripped New York, the Almanacs didn't have enough money to pay the bills, even after everyone cut way down on wine and cigarettes. They were forced to turn off the heat. Windows frosted over, pipes froze, and even multiple layers of clothes weren't enough to keep warm. Turning the gas oven on full blast, the Almanacs huddled in the kitchen, talking, eating, and singing. Woody couldn't resist whipping out a song to the tune of "Deep Ellum Blues."

> I went into the bathroom and I pulled the toilet chain,
> Polar bears on icebergs came floating down the drain.
> Hey, pretty mama, I got those Arctic Circle Blues.
> Hey, pretty mama, I can't raise no heat on you.

On December 7, 1941, the Almanacs were having one of their Sunday hootenannies when someone ran in and announced the Japanese had just attacked Pearl Harbor. Within days, America entered the war. Once again the tenor of the Almanacs songs completely changed. They stopped singing "Talking Union" and their songs became, simply, "Let's win the war."

Woody threw himself into another prolific period of songwriting. He sat for hours every night at his typewriter, changing the words to his songs, converting them into pro-war songs. He turned out anti-Hitler songs about as fast as anyone else could fix a meal. Led by Woody, the Almanacs converted their repertoire of songs so fast that they became some of the first entertainers turning out war propaganda in New York. Their music provided a strong countertempo to the melodious, swinging big bands with their overblown, sentimental lyrics and the commercial "Tin Pan Alley" songs flooding the airwaves.

Suddenly, the Almanacs were in demand everywhere. They appeared on their first network radio show and a music publisher rushed to put out an Almanac songbook. Evenings they spent running from one booking to another. Their biggest audience of all was on a program called *This Is War*, broadcast on all four radio networks simultaneously in an effort to boost national morale.

But while the Almanacs were enjoying their new popularity, the FBI was surreptitiously photocopying documents relating to the Almanacs, recording their phone calls, and infiltrating meetings. A reporter from the New York *World-Telegram* uncovered their Communist affiliations and broke the news on February 17, 1942. The Almanacs commercial success went dead overnight.

But Woody didn't care. He'd fallen wildly in love with a young dancer named Marjorie Mazia.

Marjorie Mazia (right) performs with Flier (center) and Sophie Maslow (left).

Chapter Eight
1942-1943
Folksay Dancers

"I am stormy like the weather and I do a lot
of useless tossing and whirling and pitching."

In a cold, drafty studio on Thirteenth Street a dancer named Marjorie Greenblatt Mazia was rehearsing *Folksay*, an experimental modern dance. At twenty-five, Marjorie was small, quick on her feet, and unbelievably full of energy. The dancers moved to a mixture of folk songs and spoken verses from Carl Sandburg's poem "The People, Yes." Like Marjorie, most of the performers were from the Martha Graham Dance Company.

Marjorie had been dancing with Martha Graham for just a few years, and considered herself one of the luckiest people in the world. Born on October 6, 1917, in Atlantic City, New Jersey, she was the daughter of Russian Jewish immigrants. Her mother, Aliza Greenblatt, was a renowned Yiddish poet, and her father supported the family by working in the garment business. Marjorie's father, Isidore, loved ideas, books, and art. He was a fierce debater, especially passionate about the need for a Jewish state in Palestine. Both of Marjorie's parents encouraged her in her love of music and dance, and were delighted when she joined Martha Graham's dance troupe.

Martha Graham found she had more than an enthusiastic dancer when Marjorie joined the troupe. Marjorie had a wonderful aptitude for teaching, with highly organized thinking and cheerful ways of getting the most from the dancers. Marjorie was soon leading classes in the mornings and rehearsing in the afternoons. Evenings Marjorie performed with the troupe or worked on experimental pieces like *Folksay*, choreographed by another dancer, Sophie Maslow.

In January 1942, Sophie mentioned to Marjorie that she wanted to choreograph a dance to one of Woody Guthrie's songs that she'd heard on his *Dust Bowl* album. She hoped he would appear onstage and sing his song, live, with a group of dancers. She told Marjorie that Woody was right here in New York, and she was going to go ask him personally. "I'm coming with you," Marjorie announced.

Sophie was surprised by Marjorie's quick response. But Marjorie had already fallen in love with the *Dust Bowl* album. The song Woody had composed in one night, "Tom Joad," thrilled Marjorie. When Tom must leave his family and his mother doesn't know where he's going, or how she's going to find him, he tells her:

> "Wherever little children are hungry and cry,
> Wherever people ain't free,
> Wherever men are fightin' for their rights,
> That's where I'm a-gonna be, Ma,
> That's where I'm a-gonna be."

Marjorie felt Woody had put her feelings into words, better than she ever could herself. She was mystified—how could this Okie know and express her feelings so well? She had a powerful image of Woody from his voice: a tall, strong man, striding through New York in cowboy boots and a broad-brimmed hat. She couldn't wait to meet him.

Sophie and Marjorie packed a basket of fruit for Woody and set off for the Almanac house one cold January day. One of the Almanacs let them in, and they found Woody standing in the living room, his back to them as he stared out the window. Light streamed in around him. Marjorie was shocked. Woody was small, petite even, nothing like she had imagined. His clothes were rumpled and too big for him. But when he turned around and greeted them, she was struck by his eyes. They were so honest and clear, as if everything he felt was right there. And there was something else—a vulnerability about him that was very compelling.

Woody was eager to perform with Sophie's group, but the first rehearsal was a disaster. He never sang a song the same way twice, and every time he changed his timing, the dancers went colliding into each other. The dancers insisted he sing the song exactly as he had on the record.

Woody tried not to show it, but inside the criticism was making him "fume and cuss and snort." He tried again, and once more dancers crashed into each other.

"If I want to take a breath between verses, I play a few extra chords," he said. "And if I forget the lines and want to remember them, I play a few extra chords. And if I want to get up and leave town, I get up and leave town."

Woody headed home after the rehearsal feeling defensive and frustrated. He and Marjorie walked partway home together, Marjorie heading for Fourteenth Street and Woody for the Almanac House on Tenth Street. As he walked beside Marjorie, Woody felt his frustration lifting. When they got to the corner of Twelfth Street and Sixth Avenue, he felt reluctant to part. Woody stood, surprisingly mute, then gave a quick nod. Marjorie said goodnight, and they went their separate ways.

Woody walked home thinking how young and alive and healthy and hardworking Marjorie was. He figured she was just "awful friendly and sympathetic to strangers," and that she had walked with him because she thought he was "a pitiful sight, lonesome, tangled up," and needed her cheerful company.

Woody was having a hard time, unsure just what he was doing in New York, and put off by the increasing number of people joining the Almanacs with no musical training but the right political views. Sometimes as many as eight or ten people gathered onstage, and their performances were unstructured and amateur.

"We had organizational minds, Workers' School students, Square Dance Groups, Lawyers and Writers Guild Members, and horse traders and swappers, and Fishermen and Seamen and soldiers and Photographers," Woody wrote. At the frequent Almanac House meetings, Woody argued passionately against everyone coming up onstage and singing together. He wanted to be on the stage and have them in the audience. But he was voted down.

Woody began distancing himself from the Almanacs. "I'll always believe that my gift is for telling stories with a guitar, and this is most often a one-man job." But he wasn't sure just where he was heading.

The second *Folksay* dance rehearsal didn't go much better than the first. Sophie was ready to find a new folksinger and Woody was ready to walk when Marjorie came up with a solution. She wrote out his lines on a piece of cardboard, marking out the exact pauses as well as the words. Now, more often than not, Woody could get it right, singing and chanting under his breath, "I'm goin' down the road feeling bad two three four."

With the counting problem solved, Woody relaxed and began enjoying rehearsals. He loved watching the dancers, with their lithe, confident movements. He admired how hard they worked—the strenuous evening rehearsals following a full day's classes and rehearsals for an upcoming tour with Martha Graham.

He and Marjorie gravitated toward each other over the next few weeks. During breaks, Marjorie played his songs on the piano in the rehearsal hall. Woody loved to hear how she played them, feeling that she was taking his songs—and him—to a new level. "They widen out, broaden and deepen, take on all kinds of new expression and rhythms," he confided to her later. "Back on the corner of 6th Ave., and 12th Street there that night, I suppose, something like all of this was going through my head. In other words, life was getting bigger and plainer, and shaping itself into something almost so good and healthy that I didn't dare to hope for too much of it."

As they walked or lingered in cafés after rehearsals, he told Marjorie that he'd been given an advance of five hundred dollars to write a book about his childhood. But he was struggling with it. He could write the scenes all right—his mother's illness, the gang house, the oil boom

Woody plays while Marjorie dances in the *Folksay* program, 1942.

123

hitting Okemah—it all came pouring out of the typewriter as fast as he could think. But he couldn't seem to structure the manuscript. The Almanac house was full of distractions— people coming and going at all hours, music being played, wine jugs being passed around. Marjorie was sympathetic, and once she read some of his prose, impressed. His writing was brilliant, just like his songwriting.

In early March, the troupe performed *Folksay*, with Woody sitting on the stage, playing his guitar, singing, and counting under his breath. He managed to keep his beats right, and the show went off beautifully.

After the performance, Woody glanced over his shoulder and saw Marjorie wearing his jacket. "I think I fell in love with you some more," he wrote her later, "and still it was too good to ever happen to me, so I didn't mention it." That night they walked home through the cold March night together, Woody holding her hand, gently touching her warm skin through a small hole in her glove.

Marjorie was leaving in the morning for a tour with Martha Graham, but she invited him up to her room. They sat up all night talking—Marjorie confiding her hopes and longings about expressing herself in dance, Woody telling her about all the freights he'd ridden and the places he'd been. But he still didn't have the nerve to tell her he was falling in love with her. Nor did he make a move toward her.

"I didn't want you to think that you was being followed home by a wolfer," he explained later. In the morning she rushed out to catch a train, pausing only long enough to give Woody the keys to her room, telling him he could stay there and write while she was gone. Woody immediately brought over his typewriter and had "12 of the most lonesome days and nights that I've ever spent in my life."

Marjorie sent constant postcards and letters back to Woody in her small room on Fourteenth Street, full of surprise at how deeply she had fallen in love with him. She cajoled him to take care of himself, to bathe, brush his teeth, and above all, to write steadily.

Woody sent back a stream of letters and found a way to make their separation more bearable. In the evenings, when loneliness tugged the worst at him, he'd slip into her blue robe, turn out all the lights, and walk around the room sprinkling her perfume into the air. "The movement and the nice smell has a tendency to suggest that life is still somewhere in all of this ocean of dark," he wrote. He closed his letter saying, "I give my whole life to your keeping." Neither of them had any idea just how prophetic that would turn out to be.

When Marjorie came back from her dance tour it was clear they were deeply in love, and Marjorie told him he could stay with her in her little room on Fourteenth Street. "I saved up all my nerve and strength," Woody said, "and thought up all of my best speeches and novels and articles, and lectures and treatises and essays and notes and comments and just about then I finally mustered up the nerve to say, 'You're sweet.'"

But there was a serious problem they needed to face: They were both married to other people. Woody was at least separated from Mary and moving toward a divorce. Marjorie's situation was more complicated. She and her husband, Arnold Mazia, owned a small house near Washington, D.C., where he worked as an accountant. With her heavy dance schedule in New York, Marjorie had rented her room in the city, taking the train home on the weekends. Her husband had no idea she had fallen in love with Woody.

For the moment, they refused to worry about the mess they were in. During the day, Woody worked hard on his book, *Bound for Glory*. Marjorie insisted he keep

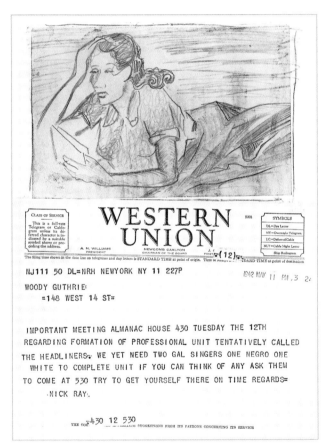

A page from Woody's scrapbooks, 1942. The sketch is probably Marjorie reading in bed.

a nine-to-five schedule, like the workers he was always so proud to sing for. He turned out the pages, and in the evenings when Marjorie got home from dancing, she helped him edit and structure his work.

In June, Marjorie told her mother, Aliza, she wanted her to meet Woody. She was sure Aliza would find him a kindred, creative spirit. The three of them met for lunch. It only took her mother a few minutes to see how Marjorie felt about Woody, and by the end of lunch she was also taken with him. Aroused by his anti-Fascist fervor, she wrote a poem in English, which she rarely did, and sent it to Woody. He promptly wrote a line-by-line critique and sent it back to her. Marjorie was delighted to see her mother, the Yiddish poet, and Woody, the Okie singer, get along so well.

Marjorie also had a secret reason for wanting the two of them to meet, a reason not even her mother guessed. She had just discovered she was pregnant, and was sure the father was Woody.

Woody and Marjorie were both thrilled. They talked and wondered and dreamed together about what kind of a child they would have: both of them highly creative, from

Woody's drawing of Railroad Pete spitting at Hitler, 1942.

such different backgrounds. Woody's imagination kicked into overdrive. Sure they were going to have a boy, Woody dubbed their child-to-be Railroad Pete and wrote frequent letters to him and Marjorie whenever they were apart. He drew dozens of pictures of Railroad Pete—a roughy-toughy kid in a slouchy hat pulled low over his eyes, his hands jammed into his pockets. Naturally, Railroad Pete was against fascism, and Woody was sure he'd grow up to be the World Champion Spitter.

Woody told everyone, with great enthusiasm, about Railroad Pete's upcoming birth. The Almanacs and Will and Herta Geer were amazed by the change that had come over Woody. Somehow, Marjorie had managed to domesticate him. He wore chinos now and his hair, if not combed, was at least clean.

As the heat of summer worsened, the Almanacs continued to limp along, but now they could go days or even weeks between paid bookings. Where they used to make $12.50 to perform, they were now paid $10.00 or even $7.50. The lack of money didn't dim Woody's anti-fascist fervor one bit. He wrote across his guitar, "This machine kills fascists," figuring his music was a vital part of the war effort.

But the strains of living together and not making any money were beginning to crack the Almanacs. Tempers flared, and political arguments took on a bitter edge. People were less tolerant of Woody's autocratic tone of voice and the way he jumped up in the middle of meetings and headed for the nearest bar when he'd had enough.

When Pete Seeger received his draft

Woody, 1943.

notice, he wrote in his journal that he was almost glad to be leaving the Almanacs before everything totally fell apart. He joined up in July, just about the same time Marjorie went up to Bennington College to teach with Martha Graham for the summer.

With Marjorie gone and the Almanacs on the skids, Woody fell into one of his lonely downward spirals. Just then his friend Cisco blew back into town after a tour with the Merchant Marine. Woody painted a vivid picture of Cisco to Marjorie, saying he "sings a high cowboy kind of coyote, snifting, drifting harmony that seems to bring a gleam of wrangling to the eyes of many girls. He's a big cuss, with a mixed walking gait that comes from being by nature a western desert rat and an expert at walking with high waves rolling against a ship."

With Cisco back in town, Woody's mood lifted. "Imagine us busting into a bottle of some kind of rum, just laughing and telling wild tales and singing and singing and singing. Together we make just about such a team as Pete and me. In fact, with Pete in the Army, I guess Cisco and me will sorta team up once in a while and sing around."

While Woody was singing and carousing with Cisco, Marjorie was thinking and planning. When she came back to New York at the end of the summer, she told Woody she couldn't bear to burden the baby with the stigma of illegitimacy. She had decided to stay with her husband, Arnold, until six weeks after the baby was born. That way the baby would be legitimate, and she and the baby could have the best possible medical care.

Woody was devastated. He'd never considered that he would have to wait months longer for Marjorie. It sent his mind spinning in a whole new direction: When was she going to tell Arnold the baby wasn't his? His worry darkened: Maybe the baby was Arnold's, and Marjorie was just trying to let him down gently. Filled with anger and self-pity, he lashed out at her: Did she even know whose baby she was carrying?

Marjorie assured him the baby was his and that she loved him and wanted to be with him. But soon she was too pregnant to dance with the troupe and had no further excuse to stay in New York. She gave up her room and moved back to live with Arnold and wait for the baby's birth.

Woody, on the fiddle, playing with Cisco Houston, 1944.

Unable to pay the rent on Marjorie's room, Woody moved in with two of the Almanacs, Gordon Friesen and Sis Cunningham, on Hudson Street. Marjorie came to visit him occasionally, but his main link with her was through letters. He wrote Marjorie and Railroad Pete long, wild letters, drew cartoons, and sent sharp, funny poems about the Fascist menace.

Time crept slowly for Woody. "I have dreams that tell me I'm not entirely as sane as is comfortable," he wrote her. "I don't know what kind of feelings are in me to cause me to write all the things I do. One minute I'm nervous and afraid and the next minute I'm as big and strong as anyone."

The same wildly disparate emotions came up with Marjorie. Sometimes he was deeply in love, delighted to see her, and at other times angry and frustrated they weren't living together. After one visit when he was especially nasty, he immediately dashed off a letter, saying that he regretted all the things he'd said. "There are red devils with pitch forks pokin around in me somewhere and making me yell out some pretty bad things. It puzzles me to even try to think how a person with a mind like yours can even stand the presence of a mind like mine."

At the end of October, Woody finished up the last changes on *Bound for Glory* and turned them in to his publisher. But bookings had just about dried up for the Almanacs. As Pete Seeger had predicted, they fell apart completely. Gordon Friesen and Sis Cunningham, tired of struggling to survive, moved to Detroit to get wartime jobs in a factory. Sonny and Brownie went back to performing together.

Forced to move again, Woody found a tiny fourth-floor walk-up on Charles Street. With a monthly rent of only twenty-seven dollars the price was right, but it was a cramped, dingy, and depressing room with no light. Woody, with his usual ironic touch, named it El Rancho del Sol.

On Sunday November 22, 1942, Woody was booked to perform with Sonny and Brownie at a big Win the War rally in Baltimore. The three of them took the train down to Baltimore and sang for several thousand people. With Baltimore on the border between the North and South, the rally organizers felt they were being quite progressive to ask blacks and whites to perform together.

After they finished singing, the chairman invited Woody to sit at the head table, and told Sonny and Brownie they would be seated at a table in the corner.

Woody went crazy. He started hollering, "Didn't you see me standing up there between

Eating together in a restaurant in New York City, 1944: Brownie McGhee and Woody are on the left, Sonny Terry is second in from the right.

those two guys all night long singing 'Union Forever'? You mean to tell me that they can't sit at this table with us? They gotta eat like two dogs in the corner? You want to talk about fascism? The fight against fascism starts right here."

He grabbed the edge of the table and flipped it over, sending glasses, silverware, and china crashing to the floor. Then he walked over to the next table and flipped it over. Brownie couldn't believe it. "Me and Sonny were terrified," he said. "Sonny couldn't see and I couldn't run. We just held on until the storm was over."

The three of them were hustled into a taxi for the ride to the train station, with Woody grumbling the whole way, "Goddamn fascists!"

Woody's longing for Marjorie continued to be almost unbearable. A week after the performance in Baltimore he wrote her: "I would give the world and all that's in it, if I owned it, to see you and talk to you right now." But as the due date for Railroad Pete crept closer, his fears compounded: "I have been letting myself entertain little old hateful and doubtful thoughts about us, and the possibility that you'll make up your mind to stay in Washington." Barely capable of anything else, he spent his time fretting and worrying.

On February 6, 1943, Cathy Ann was born. Woody rushed to the hospital, where he stood looking at his new baby daughter through the nursery window for nearly an hour. More than anything, he wanted to pick her up and hold her.

Overwhelmed with longing for Marjorie and his new daughter, Woody went home and wrote out his feelings in a seventy-page free-verse letter, including a poem to Cathy Ann.

I FELT LIKE MOST OF ALL THINGS I WANTED
   WAS TO GET A HOLT OF YOU AND TO FEEL HOW
     GOOD AND HOW SMOOTH AND HOW
       WARMSY WARMERY
          YOUR SKIN IS RIGHT
          HERE
          AND RIGHT HERE
             AND OVER YONDER

But he also had to let go of his vivid fantasy relationship with Railroad Pete. He wrote a long, complex letter in which he claimed Cathy Ann had told him she had seen Railroad Pete "many times back where I come from," and promised to carry on his anti-Fascist views.

Marjorie came for a visit and dropped another bombshell. When she came to New York in April, she wasn't going to move in with him. She planned to rent an apartment just for her and Cathy Ann, near her parents in Sea Gate. She wanted to give them a little time to get used to the idea that the baby was Woody's and she planned to marry him.

Woody went through the roof. He wrote her a long, scathing letter about how she'd been running back to her husband for over a year now, at the least provocation. He understood that the safe, financially secure life she was leading had an attraction for her.

"To me people that are in love wrap their little babies up in a rug or a blanket and cross deserts, wade swamps, cross icebergs, wade snow, do anything to be together, but it seems that you have always put a hamburger or an orange juice or your belly before any thoughts of love." He wrote bitterly that all he could say was good-bye and good luck. "I can't live insane any longer," he ended. "Your friend, Me."

Stung, Marjorie fired a letter back to Woody. "I am self sufficient and can stand on my own two feet," she wrote. "I'm still coming to New York when and how I choose. You were never much help in seeing to it that I got there. You only cried that you were helpless . . . that you were lost . . . that you were insane . . . that you were lonely . . . always you and you and you . . . Well Mr. YOU I hope you find that there are some other things in this world and they don't all begin with you. There is me and him and her."

Woody's apology was deep, abject, and instantaneous. "(Hello) (Can I sneak in for a minute?)" he began his next letter to her. Gently, earnestly, he assured Marjorie he loved her and wanted to be with her. She accepted his apology, and on April 15, Woody borrowed a car and he and Brownie brought Marjorie and Cathy Ann to New York.

BOUND
FOR
GLORY

BOUND
FOR
GLORY

WOODY
GUTHRIE

WOODY GUTHRIE

DUTTON

WOODY GUTHRIE

Chapter Nine
1943-1945

Shipping Out

"A torpedo knocks a lot of things out of you, and if you live through the shake up, it knocks a lot of new things into you. It puts a lot of your thoughts straighter in your mind, and sets your hopes and your plans up clearer and plainer."

Telling Marjorie's parents the truth was both easier and harder than Marjorie expected. Her mother wasn't surprised—she'd felt this coming since being introduced to Woody a year ago. But Marjorie's father, a devout Jew, couldn't accept that Marjorie wanted to marry a Gentile. He brutally told her that he would never set foot in their home.

Woody and Marjorie had no choice but to accept his decision, painful as it was, and begin building a life together. With Marjorie back in New York, Woody could relax and enjoy the critical success of *Bound for Glory*. Reviewers loved his book and felt that Woody's talent was enormous. Some were sure he was destined to be the next important American writer. The publisher, delighted with sales, arranged to have twenty-five dollars a week sent to Mary in Texas, and asked Woody to write another book.

Suddenly everybody seemed to want Woody. He was invited to parties all over town. If they were too fancy and he behaved badly, people laughed and excused him as eccentric. He made a number of appearances, singing and explaining how his morale-boosting songs fought fascism.

Children crowd around Woody as he plays his guitar, New York, 1943; *Bound for Glory* book jacket.

But the U.S. government thought he could fight Fascism better as an army private, and in May 1943, he was ordered to report for a physical to be drafted.

The last thing Woody wanted was to be inducted into the army. He decided to join Cisco and ship out with the Merchant Marine, which would exempt him from the draft. He and Cisco and a friend of Cisco's, Jimmy Longhi, went down to the National Maritime Union hiring hall on Seventeenth Street and signed on the *William B. Travis*, a Liberty ship hauling supplies to Europe.

The Merchant Marine was preferable to being in the army, but it was still incredibly dangerous. Hundreds of ships were moving across the Atlantic carrying bombs, food, tanks, and gasoline to Europe. Hitler, desperate to cut the lifeline of supplies coming from America, had packs of German submarines, or U-boats, patrolling the Atlantic. In March, two months before Woody signed up, the Germans had located every one of the Atlantic convoys, attacked half of them, and sunk more than 20 percent of the ships.

A few weeks after signing up, Woody kissed Marjorie and Cathy good-bye and boarded the ship. Despite the dangerous cargo on board—two-ton bombs and gasoline—Woody was exhilarated. He liked being part of all the activity, a man working with other men. It was a relief to be moving again, even if it was on ship and not thumbing down a road. And after singing for so many unions, he was now a proud member of the NMU, the National Maritime Union.

Woody was put in charge of serving meals for the twenty-man navy gun crew, which he did with varying degrees of success. He couldn't always be counted on to get the floor swept and mopped, the tables set and ready for meals, but he wrote up spectacular menus. Something as tasteless as canned beef stew became:

> Aunt Jenny's prize-winning Saturday night special made of
> choice chunks of prime Texas beef, braised in golden butter,
> cooked with 14-carat carrots, plump tomatoes, California

celery and sweet Spanish onions seasoned and stirred every 10 minutes by a beautiful virgin, if available, or by the youngest member of the gun crew.

From the first day on ship, Woody was busy even when he wasn't on duty. He sporadically wrote dozens of pages of his new novel, and long, rambling letters to Marjorie and Cathy. He carved a chess set out of a mop handle and cajoled Jimmy into singing background vocals for him and Cisco.

One night after dinner the ear-shattering sound of the general quarters alarm bell rang out. Terrified, everyone ran into the alleyway and surged up the gang ladders to the deck.

"A ship's hit!" shouted a gunner.

Navy destroyers chased up and down the outside of the convoy, letting off depth charges to try to knock out the prowling German submarines. *Whoom! Whoom!* The explosions sent huge columns of water into the air and made the metal ship reverberate.

Sailors paced nervously all over the deck, terrified their ship would be hit next. It was sickening to realize their vulnerability. If they were hit, the explosion of their cargo would probably kill them. Even if they survived the blast and were thrown into the water, they'd die of cold and exposure.

At midnight the alert was finally called off, and Woody, Cisco, and Jimmy headed to their bunks. They didn't talk about the ship that had been hit, or her crew. Lying in the dark in their bunks, it was impossible to fall asleep. They were still wound up, afraid their ship would be next.

After a few minutes, Woody spoke in the dark.

"No, I wasn't afraid," he said, as if someone had asked him a question.

He went on talking, saying the only thing that scared him was fire. He told Cisco and Jimmy about his parents' house burning down, and Clara's fiery death. The words came tumbling out of him as he told them about his mother getting worse and her death in an insane asylum.

Jimmy and Cisco heard Woody's cigarette pack rustling in the dark.

"But I'm sure that she was not insane. I'm sure she had a physical illness of some kind," Woody said, striking a match. "The talk in our family is that she inherited it.

"I'm beginning to suspect that I have it, too." The light from the match trembled as he lit his cigarette. "The doctors don't know much about it. Maybe only Jesus can help me."

He finished his cigarette in silence.

• • •

The next morning they saw an empty space where the ship behind them had been. They were now in "dead coffin corner," vulnerable to attack from German submarines on two sides.

Despite their terrible position, the ship made it across the Atlantic without being torpedoed. They unloaded the cargo in Palermo, Italy, and headed out across the Mediterranean to Tunisia. A few hours into the trip there was a huge explosion. The ship rolled violently to one side, then careened back and forth, the steel in the ship groaning. In the pitch dark, men began shouting and screaming.

Woody pushed his way into the blacked-out alleyway with all the other

Woody tried to make light of a possible explosion at sea, 1943.

terrified sailors and swarmed up to the deck. He stood next to the railing, feeling the ship's bow slowly settle lower and lower as she took on water through the hole ripped in her side. A strange, uncanny silence fell over the sailors as they waited to see if they would sink, or be hit by another torpedo.

Finally the captain gambled they could make it to port and started the engines, ordering everyone to stay on deck. Shortly after the sun came up on the rusty brown hills of Tunisia, the ship was safe in the harbor.

Woody, Cisco, and Jimmy squeezed onto a crowded Liberty ship for the trip home, and a month later they were back in New York. Woody had been gone four months and had earned eight hundred dollars.

While he was away, Marjorie had rented an apartment for them on Mermaid Avenue in Coney Island. Just one long block from the beach, the area was crammed with hot dog and cotton candy stands, penny arcades, and souvenir shops. The clatter of roller coasters filled the air, along with the shouts and laughter of summer vacationers, but during the winter everything was shut down and boarded up.

Woody and Marjorie loved to put Cathy in her stroller and walk along the wooden boardwalk, the wheels clicking rhythmically over the wooden planking, the sea breeze blowing lightly across them. Watching Woody push Cathy in her stroller one day, Marjorie noticed he was having trouble with his balance. That's funny, she thought, he must be so used to carrying his guitar that walking without it causes him problems. It wasn't until years later that she realized it was an early sign of Huntington's Disease.

Woody, home with Marjorie and Cathy, was feeling incredibly lucky to be alive. Life stretched out ahead of him, full of hope, love, and promise. He had plenty of ideas for more books, plenty more songs to write and sing.

Cathy was an unending sense of wonder to Woody. She'd grown so much while he was gone. She had curly brown hair like Woody's, a quick smile, and a clear mind about what she wanted.

Late one evening, Cisco and Jimmy came over to Mermaid Avenue for a visit. When their talking woke Cathy up in the next room, Marjorie turned on her night-light and invited them to come in and see her. "She held her eyes wide open and gave each one of us such a looking over that all of us fell under the power of her stare," Woody wrote.

Marjorie spoke softly to Cathy to let her know she was in the admiring crowd gathered around her crib. "She has come to know your voice in the sun, the fog, the rain, snow, darkness, and so have I," Woody wrote Marjorie later. "I'm pretty sure that both of us hear it, feel it, and know it wherever we are."

In early January 1944, Woody set sail again with Cisco and Jimmy, transporting war supplies and two hundred oil workers to Oran in North Africa. It was an uneventful trip, but without the magic and camaraderie Woody had found earlier. His letters to Marjorie veered into uncertainty: "I write like a big man but I feel little and small," he wrote.

By late March, Woody was back in New York. Cisco, with nowhere else to stay, slept on a cot in Cathy's room. Being together constantly gave Woody and Cisco plenty of time to practice. Without their shipboard duties, they started playing early in the morning and often didn't quit until Marjorie got home at night.

A few weeks later Woody heard about a man named Moe Asch who had a tiny recording studio on West Forty-sixth Street and was interested in recording folk songs. A burly, enthusiastic man, Asch had fallen in love with folk music years earlier when he'd first seen a copy of John Lomax's book *Cowboy Songs.*

Woody lost no time in finding Asch's office, and walked in unannounced.

"I'm Woody Guthrie," he said, squatting on the floor in front of the door.

"So?" said Asch. He'd never heard of him.

"I have a lot of songs I want to record," Woody said.

As Asch listened to Woody talking, he quickly realized that he was listening to an articulate, serious person. "The simplicity of his speech was so deep that you start to remind yourself of Walt Whitman," Asch said. "The words were clear, simple, but the meanings were deep and very well thought out and philosophized."

Asch invited Woody to record. Woody returned on April 16, 1944, and recorded a few songs. These went well, and three days later Woody returned with Cisco and Sonny Terry. In a phenomenally long session, they recorded sixty-three songs. Several more marathon sessions followed in the next few weeks.

Used to playing just with Cisco, Woody loved what Sonny added to the session.

> Sonny Terry blew and whipped, beat, fanned and petted his harmonica, cooed to it like a weed hill turtle dove, cried to it like some worried woman come to ease his worried mind. He put the tobacco sheds of North and South Carolina in it and all of the blistered and hurt and hardened hands cheated and left empty, hurt and left crying, robbed and left hungry, pilfered and left starving, beaten and left dreaming.

Happy in his New York life, Woody figured he was done with the Merchant Marine, but in May the army came after him again. Woody reluctantly signed up with Cisco and Jimmy on the *Sea Porpoise*, carrying three thousand young soldiers to Europe.

The morning they were to board, Cisco and Jimmy arrived first and waited for Woody. When he finally showed up, it wasn't surprising he was late. They could barely see him under the load he was carrying. He had "a seabag over his shoulder, a guitar strapped to his back, a violin case, a mandolin case, a stack of at least ten books, and a portable typewriter, all tied together by a length of clothesline and somehow wrapped around him."

On June 6, 1944, as the ship was crossing the Atlantic, news came over the radio that Allied troops had invaded the coast of Normandy, France. Along with thousands of others, Woody was sure that the invasion would bring a quick end to the war. But it made the crossing highly dangerous: Desperate to cut off the invading forces, German submarines patrolled the Atlantic more ferociously than ever before.

It wasn't very many days before German submarines were spotted and the general alarm bell began its ear-splitting ring. Forcing the three thousand troops to stay below, the crew was kept topside for hours as destroyers raced back and forth exploding depth charges. Finally, around nine o'clock at night the tired, nervous sailors were allowed to go below, despite the continuing general alarm. Most of the exhausted sailors grabbed the hard-boiled eggs and sandwiches set out in the mess halls and headed for their bunks.

But Woody went to his cabin only long enough to pull his guitar out from under his bunk. He headed down to the holds, where the young GIs had been cooped up all day, praying, crying, seasick and fearful, listening to the terrifying sounds of the depth charges. Cisco and Jimmy reluctantly followed Woody, sure they would die down in the holds if the ship was hit.

Standing in the middle of the number three hold, Woody tuned his guitar and launched into his song "The Sinking of the *Reuben James*," a song he'd written in January 1942, when he was with the Almanacs.

"Holy Mother," said Cisco, looking at Jimmy. Why would Woody sing a song about an American destroyer torpedoed while protecting a convoy like this?

"It's a cheerful little tune that goes rippling along nice and easy," Woody told the soldiers, who broke into nervous laughter. With his usual uncanny sense of his audience, Woody knew exactly what they needed. This was a time for Woody's dark humor. Eighty-six men had died when the *Reuben James* sunk, inspiring Woody to write a tender song in memory of those killed.

"You guys join in the chorus," he said, "and remember to sing loud, because scientists have discovered that loud singing sends out sound waves that confuse the Nazi U-boats and causes them to shoot crooked." Within minutes he had all the soldiers singing as the depth charges reverberated against the sides of the ship.

After an hour and a half they stopped for a smoke, and heard the sound of a rich, strong chorus rolling down the hall. Woody took off with his guitar, followed by Cisco and Jimmy, and found fifty black soldiers crammed into a nearby bathroom, standing on the toilet seats, sitting on the cubicles, packed in the middle of the room. They were harmonizing, heads thrown back, eyes shut. He listened to them until they noticed him standing in the doorway and stopped.

"That's about the best darn singing I ever heard," Woody told the leader. He invited them to come back and sing with him in the number three hold. The leader looked at him a minute to make sure he wasn't joking, then said they couldn't, because blacks weren't allowed in that part of the ship.

"Well, then," said Woody, "this here is where we give our next concert."

Woody playing for African-American GIs during the war.

Woody wasn't supposed to be where he was either, in the "colored toilet." The armed forces were strictly segregated, with blacks and whites in separate units—sleeping, eating, and fighting separately, with white officers commanding all-black units. If a black unit in the field became undermanned, white GIs wouldn't be sent to reinforce it. If wounded black soldiers required blood transfusions, only the plasma of other black soldiers could be used to save their lives.

But Woody never did like rules. He launched into a song, much to the discomfort of the black GIs. But before long, united by music and the threat of the German submarines prowling nearby, they were trading and swapping songs.

A white officer, hearing them singing, tried to bust them up, but Woody and Jimmy talked him into reluctantly letting them all go to the number three hold. Woody and Cisco turned out song after song, the black soldiers making a resounding chorus. The white GIs jumped up to dance, but the black soldiers sat stiffly, nervous about being in the all-white hold. The officer looked on reprovingly.

As song followed song, the terrifying thud of the depth charges was muffled in the background. The dancing got so frenzied that even the nervous black soldiers jumped to their feet to dance. Suddenly the white officer jumped up and began dancing with the most sure-footed black soldier.

It was after three in the morning before Woody, Cisco, and Jimmy got back to their cabin, exhausted and emotionally pent up. Cisco sat on the edge of his bunk strumming his guitar and softly sang Jimmy and Woody to sleep.

In early July, the *Sea Porpoise* discharged the soldiers right into the fighting at Normandy. Where there had once been three thousand eighty-five men on the *Sea Porpoise*, there were now only eighty-five. The ship seemed silent and deserted, and the air hung heavy with the painful reality that many of the young men they had been entertaining wouldn't survive the next few days.

The beach was only twenty minutes behind them when a mine ripped into the side of the *Sea Porpoise*. Incredibly, the ship managed to stay afloat and was pulled into port in

England. To commemorate surviving his second torpedoing, Woody carved on his violin "Drunk once, sunk twice."

Back home again by early August, Woody was determined to get his next book written. Marjorie made him a small plywood desk in the corner of the living room, but he had trouble settling down. He was always ready to play with Cathy or take her down to the beach. Friends dropped by with bottles of rum, wanting to play music and talk. Frustrated and angry with himself, Woody fought with Marjorie as she tried to get him to keep regular hours, eat well, brush his teeth, and put on clean clothes.

His mood improved when he was hired for a weekly radio program on WNEW. Songs started pouring out of him again, and he wrote one of his most touching songs, "1913 Massacre." He'd recently read a book by Mother Bloor, *We Are Many*, which included the story of a Christmas party for a group of striking copper workers. During the party, company thugs had yelled "fire!" then locked the doors. In the stampede to get out, children were trampled and crushed to death in front of the locked doors. Woody transformed the story into a song:

> Such a terrible sight I never did see;
> We carried our children back up to their tree.
> The scabs outside still laughed at their spree,
> And the children that died were seventy-three.

In March, Moe Asch released a three-album set of Woody's songs. But before Woody could enjoy it, the army, desperately searching for recruits, sent him another induction notice. Reluctantly, Woody headed down to the National Maritime Union. To his surprise, the Merchant Marine turned him down, saying he was listed as a Communist.

Woody had no choice. He had to serve in the army. In a supremely ironic moment, he was inducted on May 7, 1945, the same day Germany surrendered.

Sent to an army base in northern Texas, Woody tried to make the best of his situation.

Woody in the U.S. Army, 1945.

But as he ran through the obstacle course, set up his pup tent, and shot a rifle, he was acutely aware of how old he was. At thirty-two he'd seen a lot of the world, and it showed in his sun- and wind-burnt face. Most of the other inductees were young, with peach fuzz and acne. He longed for the company of other musicians and was painfully lonely without Marjorie and Cathy.

He wrote Marjorie that he wanted to marry as soon as her divorce was final, but he didn't think he was a very good deal. "These terrible, empty and hopeless storms have always been my real wife, and you should be the first to know it."

In August 1945, the Japanese surrendered and World War II was over. Woody was sure he'd be sent home in a couple of weeks. But weeks stretched out to months and Woody spiraled down into another of his deep depressions. "It seems like a hundred pound sack of frogs and snakes are tied to each of my arms, my mouth is full of rabbit hair and my brain is caught in a net it can't get out of," he wrote Marjorie. "Confused states of mind, a kind of lonesomeness, a nervousness stays with me no matter how I set myself to reading, painting or playing my guitar. Without trying to make it sound too serious, it never does get quite right in my head." For the next ten years Woody both knew and denied that Huntington's was closing in on him.

On November 6, the army granted Woody a two-week furlough, with the warning that when it was over, he was being transferred to Nevada. He and Marjorie had a quick marriage ceremony at New York's city hall, and after a short, wonderful respite with Marjorie and Cathy, he headed for Nevada.

The last weeks in the army crept by incredibly slowly. He wrote Marjorie frequent, intense letters, often beginning with deep explanations of how much he loved her, then veering off into pages of vivid erotic writing. Marjorie found them exciting, but highly embarrassing, and wasn't quite sure what to make of them.

Assuming he would be mustered out of the army soon, no one even bothered to assign him a job. He spent his time playing his guitar, writing letters, and fighting off depression. Only now he was more confused, his mind spinning strangely out of control.

He was writing to Marjorie about a movie he'd seen when suddenly the whole syntax of his letter changed. "Just dizzy," he wrote. "Woozy. Blubberdy. And scrubberdy and rustelty, tastelty. This is the soberest drunk I ever got on."

The next day, December 21, 1945, he was finally discharged from the army and free to go home.

Woody believed that getting people together to sing music was a way of fighting fascism.

Chapter Ten
1946-1947

Stackybones

"And the things you fear shall truly come upon you."

As soon as he got back to New York Woody grabbed his guitar and headed for Pete Seeger's house in Greenwich Village. He found Pete's wife, Toshi, in the basement working on the plumbing. Suddenly Pete came flying down the stairs, unslinging his banjo as he catapulted down.

Without even saying hello, their fingers started strumming and picking and they broke into "Sally Goodin." After being separated by the war, here they were, alive and playing music together. They tossed out songs to each other, moving through "Doggy Spit a Rye Straw," "Going Down This Road Feeling Bad," and "Worried Man Blues," before they finally quit.

That night at Pete's house they held a meeting of folksingers to figure out how to build a musical organization for the post-war times. All the old Almanacs came, and dozens of young earnest folksingers. After greeting each other, swapping war stories and telling jokes, they settled down to business.

Led by Pete Seeger, the group discussed the need to get back to writing and singing songs for the labor movement. After four years of wartime price controls and frozen wages, it looked like the unions would be working hard to win pay raises. Pete had huge, wildly enthusiastic plans. He was hoping to have "hundreds, thousands, tens of thousands of union choruses. Just as every church has a choir, why not every union?" He was sure unions needed singers to perform on picket lines, bring in people to meetings, and provide excitement and stirring songs for the labor movement.

The folksingers decided to form their own union and call themselves People's Songs. They'd get organized, figure out a fair price for performing, and ask for it. They'd hold hootenannies again, write new songs for the unions, and send people out to perform. To make it official, they elected officers and a board of directors, including Woody, and decided to put out a monthly bulletin.

Everyone set to work with enthusiasm, contacting unions, performing, writing songs, and putting together the People's Songs bulletin. The first bulletin opened with the stirring words, "The people are on the march and must have songs to sing. Now, in 1946, the truth must reassert itself in many singing voices." Circulation quickly topped two thousand, and People's Songs received press coverage in *The New York Times* and *Time* magazine.

Woody jumped back full-swing into his New York life. Every morning he avidly read the newspaper, wrote songs inspired by the articles, and drew quick, freewheeling sketches of what he saw in accompanying photos. He worked on his novel, spewing forth page after page, turned out articles for the monthly bulletin, and served on the People's Songs board.

On March 23, 1946, Woody, Pete, and Lee Hays flew from New York to Pittsburgh to perform for ten thousand striking Westinghouse workers. Hundreds of People's Songs bulletins were thrown from the rooftops. Filled with song lyrics, the bulletin was used by the strikers to sing along. Woody was exhilarated, filled with the "electric surge of life in the air," as they performed. "The crowd roared like the ocean in a rock cavern. Good to see and feel," he wrote.

Woody had never flown on a plane before. The land that he knew so well from tramping over the mountains, through the deserts and fields and towns, had never looked so wide and spacious. After fiddling with his seat belt and staring out the window, he scribbled out a sixteen-verse song.

Past my wing I look down
Everybody fighting about a patch of ground

I see people like the head of a pin
I can't make out the color of your skin

A little patch of green, a little patch of brown
Farm to farm and town to town

Somehow the song ended up with Pete's papers. A few weeks later Pete typed the words out and sent them to Woody with a note: "I don't know if you realized how goddamn envious Lee and I were that while we snored or fretted over one thing or another, you were writing poetry."

But while Woody and the other folksingers were writing and playing with enthusiasm, the fragile war alliance between England, Russia, and America was falling apart. Stalin warned the Soviet people that the United States and her allies posed a greater threat to the Soviet Union than Germany ever had. England's former Prime Minister, Winston Churchill, responded with an impassioned speech on the dangers of Communism spreading across Eastern Europe and threatening the West. He warned that "an Iron Curtain has descended across the Continent." The Cold War, a struggle between Communist and democratic nations that would last decades, had begun. The United States, already deeply leery of Communism, became obsessed with fear that Communism would wipe out democracy worldwide.

The FBI immediately opened a file on People's Songs, photocopying and stealing documents, recording phone calls, and infiltrating meetings. The folksingers' plans to encourage unions were highly suspicious. Besides, there were known Communist members in the group.

The FBI surveillance coincided with a purge of Communists throughout the unions. Some unions went so far as to forbid anyone associated with Communism to play for them. After enjoying incredible popularity, the folksingers found themselves unwelcome at many union rallies and strikes.

Woody had been delighted to be home and performing and writing again, but he began to falter as the months passed. He showed up drunk at meetings and performances, or skipped them altogether. When he did show up, his performances were erratic. He closed his eyes while he sang, or put indecent words to well-known songs. Sometimes he lurched onto the stage, lost track of the words to his songs, and stood swaying, strumming his guitar while he tried to pull his mind together.

Friends thought his drinking was out of control, and told Marjorie so. Marjorie agreed, and they fought angrily over his drinking. Woody refused to give in, yelling, "I've been drinking since I was four years old! I drank wine like it was water. You come from a different kind of background. That's why you feel this way!"

Hoping solitude might help, Woody rented a small room around the corner from their apartment to serve as an office. It didn't make any difference. Images and ideas rolled in and out of his mind. His novel jumped from one subject to another, never staying anywhere for long.

Anxious and frustrated, Woody wrote:

> I feel now like I have felt before, that these words are such
> a force, such a pressure, such a bomb inside me, that if I fail
> to get them out written down here . . . they will expand and
> actually explode and destroy me like wax paper.

But he didn't get them all out, at least not the way he wanted. Inevitably, he took it out on Marjorie. They'd have screaming arguments and he'd slam out of the house, taking refuge on someone's couch. Will Geer, Leadbelly, or Pete Seeger—somebody would always have room for him for a few days. When his anger had worn off he'd return home, contrite and full of promises to do better.

Marjorie would always take him back, forgiving him, understanding, wanting to make things work out. When they were apart for a few days in September, she wrote him a letter, comparing him to her dance teacher, Martha Graham.

> I have always felt that knowing her and you both so well has been the greatest lesson of my life. It is exciting and shocking to realize how organized as artists you both are, and how, in all the rest of living, there isn't the slightest sign of organization and always more complications than there should be. I want most of all to make you not just happy, but to feel full of energy and vitality.

Woody and Cathy, 1946.

The only area of his life that was a consistent pleasure to Woody was his daughter Cathy, now three years old. He had a long list of nicknames for her, calling her Stackybones, Stacky, Stackaroony, Cathy Bones, or Cathy Roony. Flipping and twisting her name and all of her nicknames around, he could call her dozens of different things in just one morning.

Though he had played with his earlier children, he'd never taken care of them for long. But Marjorie effectively enlisted his help. While she was dancing or teaching, he would sometimes walk Cathy to nursery school, then pick her up when school was out for the day. When Cathy was sick she'd stay home with Woody while he tried to get some writing done and take care of her at the same time.

Cathy fascinated Woody. She was so clever, so thoughtful, so fast and agile with her strong dancer's legs

Marjorie and Cathy at the beach, 1946.

and head of curly dark hair. Woody would listen to her talking and write down long strings of her conversation. "I've been playing and singing songs I made up now for nearly Twenty years and Cathy at 3 ½ already can out ryme, outplay, and outsing me any old day."

Woody took her words and made them into songs, claiming he was just writing down songs she gave him. A simple request from her, "Let's go riding in the car," would roll and twist in his mind, coming out later as series of childlike verses touting the joys of a car ride. In between the words Woody made wild sound effects: wordless melodies that buzzed as if he were playing a Jew's harp, the clickity-clack of doors opening and closing, even the *ah-rooga!* of the car's horn.

And the incessant childhood question "Why, Daddy?" teased and tugged at Woody until he wrote a nonsensical song called "Why Oh Why." He started with common questions, then moved on to odder and odder questions, like Why can't a bird eat an elephant? He ended each verse with the nonsensical refrain

> Why, oh why, oh why, oh why?
> Why, oh why, oh why
> Because, because, because, because,
> Good-bye, good-bye, good-bye.

As he watched Cathy doing everyday things—bathing, eating, walking down the street—more songs formed in his mind. He took ordinary childhood activities and made them into beautiful, playful songs like "Howdido?" about a child greeting people throughout the day.

> You stick out your little hand
> To every woman, kid and man,
> And you shake it up and down,
> Howdido? Howdido?
> And you shake it up and down, Howdido?

Though many of his friends thought they were mindless, unimportant tunes, Moe Asch was delighted by them, and invited Woody to the studio to record them.

Rather than the free-flowing sessions that characterized his earlier recordings, these were more serious. Marjorie came with him, orchestrating the sessions tightly, telling Woody to see Cathy in his mind while he sang to make his songs meaningful.

When they had recorded enough to release an album, Asch commissioned Woody to do a new project. He wanted a series of songs on Sacco and Vanzetti, two Italian immigrants who had been convicted of murder twenty years earlier and put to death. The two were avowed anarchists and many people thought the evidence used to convict them was weak and inconclusive.

Woody jumped into the project with a burst of enthusiasm, sure these would be the most important group of songs he ever worked on. In the summer of 1946 he put together some songs and recorded them with Asch, but he was dissatisfied and his spirits plummeted. He fired off a letter to Asch, telling him they should just forget about the project. "I'm drunk as hell today, been that way for several days," he wrote. "I refuse to write these songs while I'm drunk and it looks like I'll be drunk for a long time."

But then came some good news that cheered Woody up: Marjorie was pregnant again.

Woody was delighted and began filling his journal with letters to the new Railroad Pete. Cathy made drawings and homemade presents for the "new baby inside of Mommy's tummy."

On Thursday, February 6, 1947, Cathy turned four and celebrated her birthday in a new pink dress. A few days later she put on her birthday dress and new red sandals. She and Marjorie walked over to Sea Gate to have lunch with Marjorie's parents.

Shortly after they left, Woody took off for Elizabeth, New Jersey, to sing for the electrical workers at Phelps-Dodge. It was a crisp, sunny day, and Woody was in high spirits: The electrical workers wanted him to help celebrate the end of their eight-month strike.

When Marjorie and Cathy returned home in the afternoon, Cathy sat on the couch listening to the radio. A sudden, worrying thought crossed Marjorie's mind: Was she getting enough vitamin C for the baby? She told Cathy to answer the phone if it rang, and hurried downstairs and across the street to the fruit stand.

She wasn't gone more than five minutes, but when she returned, smoke was billowing out the front door of the apartment house. Desperate to get to Cathy, Marjorie pushed her way into the smoke-filled hall, where she saw the teenage boy from upstairs holding Cathy in his arms, partially wrapped in a blanket.

Cathy was still alive, whimpering and only partly conscious. The pink dress was burnt away, her whole body seared except her face. As Marjorie looked at her beloved daughter she thought, Please, God, let her die. Don't make her suffer.

An ambulance rushed Marjorie and Cathy to the hospital. While Marjorie sat in the waiting room, stunned and unbelieving, doctors started an IV in Cathy's ankle. Friends gathered as nurses wrapped her in bandages.

Woody had no idea what was going on at home. He stuck around at the Phelps-Dodge party for hot dogs and beer after the meeting, and bought Cathy a couple of balloons. Rather than heading home when he got back to New York, he dropped by Asch's office, and they went out for dinner to talk over a few ideas for more kids' songs.

As Woody headed home, Asch picked up an evening paper and read about Cathy's fire. He called the hospital immediately and talked to Marjorie, assuring her Woody would soon be there.

The apartment house was still full of the smell of smoke when Woody walked in about eleven-thirty. Stuck to his door was a note: "Come to the Coney Island Hospital at once." A neighbor, hearing him come in, told him, "Your little girl was burned. Go quick."

Woody flew down the stairs and into a taxi. He tried to figure out what had happened. He imagined that Cathy had lit one of the burners on the stove, or played with a book of matches on the bed. Everything he thought of he told the taxi driver, who talked with him and kept him from falling apart.

At the hospital, Woody found Marjorie in the waiting room. She clung to him, crying, and told him what had happened. Inside the emergency room, doctors and nurses changed Cathy's bandages while she screamed in pain.

Woody and Marjorie spent the night on a bench in the waiting room, Marjorie sitting up and Woody stretched out with his head in her lap. Friends came and went. Marjorie's mother sat anxiously with them. In the morning, the waiting room filled with friends and family, Cathy died.

Back in their empty apartment that afternoon, Woody prowled though the rooms looking for the cause of the fire. It was not the stove, which hadn't been touched, or his matches, sitting on their shelf. The couch, end table, and a little bit of the wall were singed, but nothing else was burnt. Sparks from the cheap wiring on the radio had started the fire.

Later that afternoon Marjorie's parents came to the house, her father for the first time. "I don't want you here when my children are dead," Marjorie cried. "I want you here when they're alive!"

That evening Cisco and Jimmy came by and took Woody for a walk on the beach. The three men, who had been through so much together, walked silently next to the steadily breaking waves.

Suddenly Woody threw himself down in the sand. A deep, agonized howl started in his throat, then grew until it seemed to fill the sky and wash out across the breakers.

After a long time, Woody got up and brushed himself off. The three men continued their silent walk across the sand.

A few days later Woody wrote in his notebook, "And the things you fear shall truly come upon you."

Chapter Eleven
1947-1952
Alcohol and Fists

"You've found something
Something I missed
You found a gladness being here
So far, I haven't found that
I found a drifting wind and a blowing rain"

Cathy's death seemed to confirm Woody's worst fear: Fire would destroy everyone, everything that he loved. He hid away in the apartment, writing letters to everyone who'd sent him a condolence note, signing them, "Cathy, Marjorie, Woody and Pete (on his way)." He wrote a long, complex poem to the boy upstairs who'd tried to save Cathy, thanking him for busting in through the door and wrapping Cathy in a blanket to stop the flames:

> I just hope and pray and keep on hoping and praying that no
>   such fires
> Will ever strike at your house and at your home, nor at your
>   family
> Like it has hit my family now several such times in odd and
>   funny ways
> And took some away from us and left others of us flat on their
>   backs in bed

> Through the days of sunshine, sleet, wind, snow clouds,
> drifting storms,
> Through the night hours down through every page of your
> calendars seasons.

But finally all the letters were written and Woody was at a loss, staggered by his grief and despair, unable to move. In the stack of condolence notes was a telegram from the Bonneville Power Authority asking if he could sing at a convention April 21. Woody had ignored the telegram when it had come just days after Cathy's death, but as the weeks passed it began to look like a good idea to head back to Oregon, where he'd composed so many fantastic songs in a creative flurry.

Woody left with Marjorie's blessings. She thought the trip might help him clear his mind. At first, Woody was exhilarated to be back on the road. He took a Greyhound bus to Spokane, Washington, where he performed for the convention, headed down to the San Francisco Bay Area, then moved on to Los Angeles. But as he worked his way south, his spirits plummeted. From Los Angeles he wrote Marjorie, "Homesick. Lonesome. Miserable and every other thing that is lousy and no good."

Waiting for Woody to come home, Marjorie was deeply depressed. She resolutely refused to blame herself for Cathy's death, telling a friend she couldn't go on if she thought that way. But the loss was staggering. In the evenings Marjorie kept thinking she heard Cathy humming and talking to herself in her bed in the next room. During the day when she was out, the sound of a crying child would make Marjorie whirl toward the sound, sure for just a moment it was Cathy crying. "Oh, Daddy," she wrote Woody, "will we ever be able to enjoy kids again?"

Woody's spirits dropped even further reading her letters. Lost and lonely, he abruptly headed home—back to Marjorie and the little apartment on Mermaid Avenue.

Waiting for the next "Railroad Pete" to be born, Woody struggled with a futile feeling that nothing mattered. He plunged deeply into the biblical stories of the Jewish exodus:

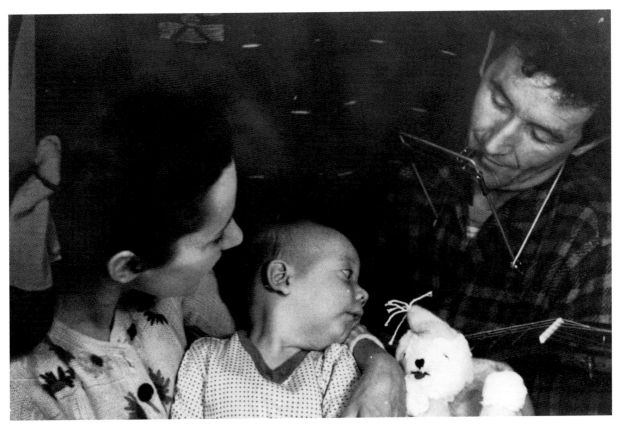

Marjorie, baby Arlo, and Woody, in 1947. It's hard to tell if Woody just happens to be tipping his head or if this is an early sign of Huntington's Disease. Notice how similar he looks in the 1958 photo taken in Greystone Park (page 190) when the disease was more advanced.

stories of loyalty, faith, and powerful heroes who saved their people from terrible oppressors. He found a copy of *The Rubáiyát of Omar Khayyám*, the eleventh-century Persian poet, which he hadn't read since his days with Lefty Lou.

As he read, he jotted notes in the margins of the pages and worked over the materials in his mind until they turned into songs, recording them with Cisco at Asch's studio. He struggled to focus his mind long enough to write other things, but was often unsuccessful. "There is some kind of an ache that comes over my hands on days when I don't write the things that I should," he noted in his journal. "And tonight I feel this ache all over me."

On July 10, 1947, four days before Woody's thirty-fifth birthday, Arlo Davey was born. It was a surprisingly hard transition for Woody, having the demands of a new baby and losing Marjorie's full attention. A month after Arlo's birth he and Marjorie had a bitter fight, and Woody angrily stormed out of the apartment. Later he wrote in his journal, half to himself and half to Marjorie, "Today I slammed my door with hate and the wind blew back acrost little Arlo . . . and you cried all morning till I opened that same old door with love."

Even Marjorie didn't realize how difficult life was becoming for Woody as the unacknowledged Huntington's came at him in waves, worsening and then retreating. "I am soft and scared and nervous and blind and feel staggery," he confessed in his journal.

In December, Woody was offered a hundred dollars to sing for the striking tobacco workers in North Carolina. He jumped at the chance, and quickly whipped out a picketline song celebrating blacks and whites working together.

The union was strictly segregated, however, and the white workers threatened to boycott his performance unless Woody cut the offending verses. Naturally Woody refused, and sang it the way he wrote it. "It cut me to my bones to have to play and sing for these Negroes with no other colors mixing in," he wrote.

Still furious over the union boycott, Woody read a newspaper article in early 1948 about a plane full of migrant workers crashing in the California hills as the Mexican workers were being deported. Woody was incensed that the article didn't even include the names of the dead workers, and came up with a beautiful song, "Plane Wreck at Los Gatos (Deportees)."

> Goodbye to my Juan, goodbye Rosalita,
> Adios mis amigos, Jesus y Maria
> You won't have your names when you ride the big airplane
> And all they will call you will be deportees.

At about the same time, he received a letter from Lefty Lou's younger sister, Mary Ruth, telling him that his cousin Jack Guthrie had died of tuberculosis. Woody immediately wrote back, full of sympathy, but then veered off into a long, disjointed pornographic letter.

People's Songs flier advertising a concert.

Perhaps Mary Ruth would have disregarded the letter if Woody hadn't followed it with two more, drawing across the pages in bright, blood-red paint. Frightened and repulsed, she decided to press charges against Woody for sending obscene material through the mail.

"If these letters had been letters of hate, I would feel guilty of every crime in the pages of our law books," he wrote the judge. "These letters are not hate letters, they are all and every word of them love letters." The judge was not moved, and decided Woody would have to stand trial.

Waiting for the trial, Woody was filled with a fresh determination to finish his manuscript. He sat for hours every day at the typewriter, handwrote across the backs of old pages, even scrawled on paper bags from the grocery store. But his determination was undermined by his drinking, now more heavy than ever. "I stumbled and fell down amongst my songs and papers," he wrote later, "dogdrunk deaddrunk and so messed up in general that I was afraid to look any earthly human in the face, and more afraid to look them in the eye."

And a strange thing was happening to his writing. He started playing with words in funny, stuttering, rhyming ways—traits he'd had before, but now they came spewing out of him, as if he almost couldn't hold them down to normal anymore, even if he wanted to. "Take it easy, but take it," became "Zakey teasy, butty zake it."

He signed his name "WWWW Gee Gee Gee Gee" or "I, Me, Woody Guthrie." His handwriting, always so neat, grew larger and loopier. Sometimes he wrote right off the edge of the paper.

On Christmas day, 1948, Marjorie gave birth to a second son, Joady Ben. Woody and Marjorie named him in tribute to Tom Joad, the main character in *Grapes of Wrath*. Despite the increased demands on his time, Woody kept working on his manuscript, determined to finish it and turn it in to the publisher.

Early in May 1949, terrible news swept through the folk music community. Leadbelly, giving a concert tour in France, had been diagnosed with Lou Gehrig's Disease, a degenerative nerve disease that gradually robs its victims of the ability to walk, talk, and use their

Leadbelly playing in concert, 1946.

arms. Like Huntington's, Lou Gehrig's is progressive and fatal, but it moves more quickly. Woody was devastated by Leadbelly's diagnosis, but the two of them carried on with a June appearance in Chicago when Leadbelly returned. It would be one of Leadbelly's last shows, as the disease was progressing rapidly.

Leadbelly was deeply ashamed to be losing control of his body and didn't want the audience to see him using a cane. "Let me walk on stage," he said. "I'll sit down then you open the curtain for me. Okay?" After the performance they drew the curtains closed as Leadbelly sat in his chair holding his beloved twelve-string guitar, then he struggled off stage.

A few months later, Woody finally delivered his manuscript—now 842 pages long—to the publishing house. The editor decided it was too long, unwieldy, often impossible to follow. He told Woody sorry, but they weren't willing to publish it.

Discouraged and depressed, Woody scrawled across an old sheet of wrapping paper:

> Could have been an artist
>   to say some good—
> But not no more
> Nope not no more
> Not anymore

In November 1949, with Marjorie eight months pregnant, the charges against Woody for sending obscene mail finally came to trial in New York. The judge listened carefully, then asked Woody if he regretted what he had done. Absolutely not, Woody replied. It was his right as an American to say or write anything he pleased. The judge promptly sentenced him to 180 days in jail.

Woody didn't mind going to jail—in fact, he was looking forward to it. He'd have a quiet routine, and time to write, maybe start something new. But Marjorie was furious with the judge for slapping Woody with such a long sentence. Here she was, eight months pregnant, needing Woody's help with Arlo and Joady when she had the new baby. Fortunately he was released early, and on January 2, 1950, he drove Marjorie to the hospital, where Nora Lee Guthrie was born.

Life in the little apartment on Mermaid Avenue reached a critical point with a newborn, a one-year-old and a two-and-a-half-year-old. After a noisy, tiring day, when all three children were tucked into bed, Marjorie and Woody still had twenty-four bottles to

Woody on a park bench in Coney Island with three of his children: Arlo, Joady, and Nora, 1953. Their apartment building is behind them.

clean and remake, and thirty-six dirty diapers to wash and rinse by hand. It wasn't the same as it had been with Cathy. Now there were just too many kids, too many needs to be taken care of night and day.

Like his mother before him, Woody found comfort in ducking out and going to the movies. There was something soothing in the darkness of the movie theater where the outside world could fade away, leaving only the predictable film.

Woody's favorite actress was Ingrid Bergman. He saw her in as many of her films as he could, such as *Saratoga Trunk, Notorious, Joan of Arc,* and *Rage in Heaven.* He'd leave Marjorie a note: "Out with Ingrid. Be home soon, I hope." He built up such an intense relationship with Ingrid in his mind he finally wrote her a tender, erotic love song.

> Ingrid Bergman, you're so perty,
> You'd make any mountain quiver
> You'd make fire fly from the crater,
> Ingrid Bergman

About the time Woody had been serving his sentence in jail, Pete Seeger was forming a new group, the Weavers, with three other musicians: Lee Hays, Fred Hellerman, and a brilliant young alto named Ronnie Gilbert. Instead of pro-union songs, they sang folk songs from all over the world. Through Pete's friend Harold Leventhal, they hired a manager who booked them into nightclubs and concert halls.

Woody, considered too unpredictable and difficult, was not asked to join. He retaliated by calling them the "Weaverlies," insinuating they were veering away from their political beliefs and had sold out by forming a popular group.

He was right about their popularity. The Weavers were more wildly popular than anyone could have guessed. In tribute to Leadbelly, who had died in December, the group closed every concert with his song "Goodnight Irene," releasing it on the "B" side of their first single record. By the spring of 1950, just months after Leadbelly's death, "Irene" was the most popular song of the year and was being played on radio stations everywhere.

No one was more surprised than the Weavers. Suddenly they had their choice of night-club bookings across the country, headlining at top places like Ciro's in Los Angeles and the glitzy clubs in Reno. And the money was unbelievable—at the Strand Theater in New York they were paid more than two thousand dollars a week.

When the Weavers asked if they could record "So Long It's Been Good to Know Yuh,"

The Weavers: Pete Seeger, Ronnie Gilbert, Lee Hays, and Fred Hellerman.

Woody was glad to oblige, despite his political feelings. He and Marjorie could use the money. He happily hunkered down on the floor and rewrote the verses on a huge sheet of wrapping paper, taking out the dust and making it more of a cheerful love song.

In November 1950, Woody was given the staggering advance of ten thousand dollars for "So Long." The money came at a perfect time. A few months earlier, fed up with living with three kids in the tiny Mermaid Avenue apartment, Marjorie had found a new apartment nearby.

For the first time, Woody and Marjorie had a real bedroom, with a separate room for the three kids. There was even a large closet they set up as Woody's writing room. Thanks to the advance, they were able to pay off their debts and buy a new car. There was even enough money for Marjorie to pursue her own dream and open the Marjorie Mazia School of Dance.

The popularity of the Weavers caused a surge of interest in all folksingers, and word spread that Woody Guthrie was one of the greatest ballad-makers alive. People listened to his albums with renewed interest, and one music producer, Howie Richmond, offered to publish and promote Woody's songs, giving him an open-ended stipend of twenty dollars a week. Richmond loved the power of Woody's lyrics, and found they made him feel surprisingly patriotic. He thought some of Woody's songs, like "This Land Is Your Land," and "Pastures of Plenty," might become the next songs that would be sung by American schoolchildren across the country.

But Woody wasn't able to perform his songs, for Richmond or anybody else. By now it was clear to everyone that there was something seriously wrong. He wandered aimlessly around town, slipping in and out of movie houses, showing up at people's homes at all hours, and having long, fractured discussions with anyone who would talk with him.

Everyone assumed he was drinking himself into the ground. His lurching walk was more obvious, and he sometimes had to reach out and steady himself on a friend, a wall, or the edge of a table. His speech was slurred and he rambled on, pointlessly.

Some people, like Asch, were furious with Woody for wasting his talent. Pete, never able to change Woody's behavior, was moving on with his career and didn't have a lot of time for this swaying, slurring shadow of his former colleague.

There wasn't much Marjorie could do either. No amount of pleading by Marjorie kept Woody's appearance reasonable. He let his hair grow wild, wouldn't change into clean clothes, and refused to wear underwear or socks.

What concerned Marjorie more was a strange warp in Woody's anger. One day in the middle of a fight, he suddenly grabbed a knife and charged at her with it. When she screamed "Woody!" he dropped the knife and seemed to come back to his senses, but it left Marjorie feeling anxious. They had always had stormy arguments, but this was different, and more frightening.

In February 1951, Woody's appendix ruptured and he was rushed to the hospital for emergency surgery. As he was recovering, one of his visitors was a young folksinger named Ramblin' Jack Elliott. A dentist's son from Brooklyn, Ramblin' Jack had fallen in love with a romanticized version of the Old West and dressed in a cowboy hat and boots. He'd seen Woody perform at a hootenanny and asked Woody to teach him "Hard Travelin'."

Ramblin' Jack Elliott and Woody in Washington Square Park, New York City, 1951.

"You can steal whatever you like," Woody replied, "but I'm not going to give it away."

Ramblin' Jack had an incredible ear, and he set about stealing Woody's songs as fast as he could. Before long, Jack could sing many of them, sounding uncannily like Woody.

Flattered and intrigued, Woody took Ramblin' Jack under his wing. He brought him along to parties and Weavers performances, and let him hang out at the apartment.

Marjorie watched fearfully as Woody's moods fluctuated from intense self-hatred to wildly grandiose self-importance. Even the children seemed wary of him, carefully tracking his moods and staying away from him when he seemed angry and out of control. One day Nora, now more than a year old, toddled over toward Woody, asleep on the couch. Suddenly she stopped and wouldn't go a step closer. Watching her, Marjorie suddenly realized the seriousness of Woody's condition. He wasn't drunk, he wasn't doing anything but sleeping, and somehow even their baby daughter was viscerally afraid of him.

It wasn't long before Marjorie decided she couldn't raise three healthy children with Woody in the house. When he took off for Florida in November 1951, she told Woody he shouldn't come back to the apartment. Woody didn't believe her—they'd had so many fights, and she'd always forgiven him and taken him back.

But this time Marjorie meant it. After visiting a friend who lived in an abandoned bus in the Florida swamp, Woody returned to New York and showed up on Marjorie's doorstep. She refused to let him in, and they drove around town, tensely talking in the car.

Marjorie had decided the only way to convince Woody she was serious was to start seeing another man. She told him she was dating Tony Marra, a big, burly Italian who was her auto mechanic.

Woody was insanely jealous. He left, sleeping on friends' couches until he'd totally worn out his welcome, then rented a cheap room. He wrote Marjorie, "I'll spend the rest of my life trying my level best to displease you in every earthly way I know."

As the weeks passed, Woody sent dozens of letters to Marjorie, berating her for seeing Tony, then switching tactics and begging her to take him back. On May 13 he wrote,

"Please come back to me Marjorie. Be my helping hand again. Please don't let me die again. Woody once again."

Two days later Marjorie came home late and found Woody waiting for her in the apartment. The children were asleep, and he'd sent the baby-sitter home. Marjorie was uneasy, but relieved to see Woody hadn't been drinking.

Suddenly all the blood drained from Woody's face and he threatened to kill her. Ranting incoherently, he beat her with his fists, then grabbed a pair of scissors. His lips were drawn back, and foamy spit ran down his chin. Praying that Woody wouldn't hurt their children, Marjorie broke free, ran to the neighbors, and called the police.

By the time they arrived, Woody was calm again and agreed to check himself into an alcohol treatment program. Early the next morning Marjorie drove him to the hospital.

The admitting nurse asked him what religion he was.

"All," he answered.

"Please don't kid around," the nurse said. "Just tell me what religion you are."

"All or none," Woody responded.

Woody was sure alcohol was his problem, his only problem. "I wish you'd grab my next bottle out of my hand and break it over my head," he wrote Marjorie. "To kick me out the door like you do (when I need help most of all) does not help."

For the next few months Woody went in and out of several hospitals, but no one knew what was wrong with him. On July 15, 1952, the day after his fortieth birthday, Woody was released and went back to his little rented room.

It wasn't long before he turned up one evening at Marjorie's. She cautiously let him in to see the children. At first everything seemed fine, but when they kept playing after being told to go to bed, Woody suddenly went berserk, going after them with his fists.

Woody was sickened and deeply ashamed. He meekly checked himself back into an alcohol treatment program the next morning. In the months to come, he wrote about the evening over and over again, begging his children for forgiveness.

I'll never lose my temper again in that old alcohol stuff that drove me to hit you that night (like I did) because you wouldn't go to sleep in your bed, remember? I remember it now so plain that it hurts me now even worse than it hurts you. That's the worst mistake I ever made in my born days. I regret it to my last day. I regret it. I do regret it. Forgive me for it. Forget it ever did happen. Let me forget that I got so angry that night and hit you so hard. We'll both forget it, won't we? We'll both pretend it never did happen, won't we? Yes we will. Yes, we will.

Marjorie needed to come up with a solution, fast. It was clear she couldn't have Woody walking out of alcohol treatment programs and showing up at the apartment, violent and out of control. She found a program she thought might help and talked it over with Woody. On July 22, 1952, Woody voluntarily transferred to Brooklyn State Hospital.

In the weeks that followed, a series of doctors examined Woody but weren't able to settle on a diagnosis. He spent his nights listening to the screaming and shouting of other men on the ward, and his days sitting at a table, turning out hundreds of pages of letters and journal entries. "Here's my funny old feeling over me again," he wrote. "That lost feeling . . . out of control, jumpy, jerky, the least little thing knocks my ego down below zero mark. Everything cuts into me and hurts me several times more than it should."

Finally a consulting neurologist examined him on September 3 and realized that Woody had a classic case of Huntington's. In stark capital letters a diagnosis was typed into his chart.

PSYCHOSIS ASSOCIATED WITH ORGANIC
CHANGES IN THE NERVOUS SYSTEM WITH
HUNTINGTON'S CHOREA.

Unbelievably, no one told Woody what the neurologist had found. Woody was left to wonder, trying to put together his increasingly strange and difficult symptoms. On September 12, feeling a dizzy spell come on, Woody headed for the bathroom and stared at his face in the mirror.

> Face seems to twist out of shape. Can't control it. Arms dangle all around. Can't control them. Wrists feel weak and my hands wave around in odd ways I can't stop . . . Awful afraid of people seeing me break down. Try to stall it off and act different. All these docs keep asking me about how my mother died of Huntington's Chorea. They never tell me if it's passonable or not. So I never know. I believe every doctor ought to speak plainer so us patients can begin to guess partly what's wrong with us . . . If it's not alcohol which has me, I wonder what it's going to be . . .

Several weeks later they finally told Woody the truth: He had Huntington's, just like his mother. Woody's reaction was immediate. He wrote a letter asking to be discharged. Since he'd voluntarily signed himself in, the staff had to discharge him, but noted in his chart, "Ultimate prognosis is poor."

Woody ran as far from the hospital as he could, as far from Marjorie and the kids, and the looming threat of Huntington's. He didn't stop running until he made it all the way to California.

Anneke and Woody, 1953.

Chapter Twelve
1952-1954
Last Run for Freedom

"I want to rest my heavy head tonight
On a bed of California stars
I'd like to lay my weary bones tonight
On a bed of California stars"

By the time Woody headed west, Americans were in a frenzy about Communist subversion, and "blacklisting" was closing in on entertainers everywhere. With Pete Seeger considered a high-profile Communist, leaks from the FBI files and testimony from informers destroyed the Weavers. "We had started off singing in some very flossy nightclubs," said Pete. "Then we went lower and lower as the blacklist crowded us in. Finally, we were down to places like Daffy's Bar and Grill on the outskirts of Cleveland." Even there, people pressured Daffy to cancel the Weavers. "Hell, no," replied Daffy. "It's just music. Quit hassling me or I'll get my boys on you."

In Los Angeles, Will Geer hit the blacklist and was unable to find work as an actor. He and Herta settled into a house in nearby Topanga Canyon, determined to wait things out. They had plenty of company. Topanga Canyon, an untamed part of the steep coastal mountains, was full of Bohemians, unemployed actors, musicians, and writers. Cisco was living nearby, and the Weavers were in the area, having found a booking at a small club in Los Angeles.

Woody showed up and was welcomed enthusiastically. Will and Herta took him in, letting him stay in a small shack on their property. Without the stress of New York, Woody's jumpy tics calmed down to trembles, the lurching walk lessened, and his slur diminished. Happy to be free and among friends, he spent hours every day writing with renewed vigor. One of the first songs he wrote in Topanga Canyon, "I Aint Dead," made a defiant announcement to the world.

> I stumble an' fall and roll and crawl
> In thornybushes like I said
> I'm all bawl'd up and all fowled up
> But still folks I aint dead
>
> I aint dead! I aint dead!
> I aint dead! I aint dead!
> I aint dead folks!
> I aint dead!

Once again denying the seriousness of his condition, Woody sent confident, optimistic letters to Marjorie: "It will all wear off, little by little, day by day; I feel my dissssy spppells a bit around here but not as dizzzzery."

In the evenings people gathered, usually at Will and Herta's house, for impromptu hootenannies. Young folksingers from all over came, eager to sing with Woody Guthrie.

One night Pete got the group improvising verses to "Acres of Clams" and Woody fired off the best version of the evening. He sang about being visited by a man from the FBI who wanted to ask a few questions.

> He asked "Will you carry a gun for your country?"
> I answered the FBI, "Yay!

I will point a gun for my country,
But I won't guarantee you which way!"

Someone told Pete there was a young woman named Odetta in the room who really knew how to sing Leadbelly's songs. He had to hunt to find her, as she was shyly sitting in the farthest corner of the room. But when she was persuaded to sing, everyone was knocked out by her rendition of the driving rhythmic Leadbelly song "Take This Hammer."

"Power, power, intensity, and power!" Pete said, awed by her voice.

Odetta and her guitar under a locust tree in California.

Woody was so sure he had a new lease on life in Topanga Canyon that he put a down payment on a steep lot with a little area flat enough to pitch a tent. He dug a cooking pit and began making his own chili beans and coffee over the open fire. One day the fire marshal tracked him down by following his plume of smoke, and told him to stop. Woody was angry and wanted to know what was the point of having land if you couldn't build a fire?

The fire marshal held firm. The last thing he needed was this long-haired, trembling Bohemian starting a forest fire in the leafy canyon. Woody was forced to move back to Will and Herta's, where he cooked his meals in the kitchen.

Woody wrote constantly, borrowing a typewriter, or writing longhand in pens and pencils, dropping one in midsentence to pick up another. A potter in the canyon invited Woody to work in his studio with clay. Woody loved the studio—once again he found an enclosed, quiet space where he could focus on just one thing. But he soon had a distraction in the studio: a beautiful twenty-year-old woman named Anneke Marshall, married to an aspiring actor. It wasn't long before Woody and Anneke were meeting at the studio and taking long walks in the wintry California sun.

Anneke loved how gentle Woody was with people and animals, and thought he was incredibly sensual, with beautiful, tender hands and a perfect body. She didn't mind the tics and lurching walk, or his rambling way of talking. It just seemed like part of who he was.

Shortly after Christmas, 1952, Anneke admitted to her husband that she was in love with Woody, and two days later she and Woody took off for New York. They only stayed a few days, long enough to meet up with Ramblin' Jack and head to Florida in his car.

Woody directed Ramblin' Jack to his friend's encampment in the swamp, but he had cleared off, leaving behind the abandoned bus. Ramblin' Jack didn't stay long, but Woody and Anneke settled into the bus. They got by on small royalty payments being sent to Woody, supplemented by a few dollars Anneke earned picking rutabagas in a neighbor's field. Woody wrote Marjorie constantly and worked on new songs, his erratic mind covering everything from the nearby alligator farm to a flood in the North Sea.

Woody in the Florida swamp, 1953.

On the morning of June 10, Woody and Anneke began preparations to relight their cooking fire. Woody filled a small can with gas and poured some into the fire pit.

The gas hit live embers hidden under the ashes. Flames arched up the stream of gas and engulfed Woody's hand. Instead of dropping the can, Woody lurched back, splashing gas up his arm. Anneke watched in horror as fire shot up to his shoulder. Woody threw himself on the ground, rolling and screaming in pain. Anneke grabbed the margarine and spread a huge handful on his burnt, dirt-covered arm, but his skin just came off in her hands like a long glove.

With Woody in shock and whimpering with pain, they rode the bus to the clinic in Jacksonville, where he was refused treatment, hospital personnel saying he lived in the wrong county. He and Anneke were sent on to nearby St. Augustine, where Woody was treated with skepticism. The doctor wrote in his chart, "The patient is peculiar—He wears shaggy hair and beard which he says is to keep mosquitoes away. This couple are drifters—came down here several months ago. Pt. is supposed to be a musician—folk musician—has quite a history."

In the days that followed, Woody's arm infected, pus oozing out from under the bandages and giving off a cloying, sickly sweet odor. Anneke realized it would be nearly impossible for him to heal in the hot, moist swamp, and they decided to head back to Topanga Canyon. Anneke had another reason she wanted to get back to civilization: She'd discovered she was pregnant. She and Woody would soon have a baby to care for.

Borrowing money from her family, they took a bus west, stopping in Mexico to file for quick divorces from their spouses. In Topanga Canyon, Anneke found a job working for the phone company, leaving Woody alone all day.

This was not the optimistic, defiant Woody who had run to California a year and a half earlier. His right arm stiffened as it healed, and he could barely strum the guitar. The curse of fire had hit once again, terrifying him, throwing him into a deep, lonely depression. Making things worse, the Geers had gone back to New York, and the evening hootenannies had been disbanded.

Woody wrote Marjorie and the kids constantly, begging them to respond. Marjorie helped Arlo and Joady, now six and five, to write back. Joady asked, "When are you going to get better, a little better, and come back to your hospital?" Arlo's letters were more direct and intense: "Woody, I love you so much. I can't stop it."

In December, with Anneke six months pregnant, they married, and Woody talked Anneke into heading for New York. Full of dreams, he thought maybe he'd be able to get something going there again. Hootenannies, recordings, maybe he'd even tour as "America's Greatest Balladeer."

They found a tiny apartment on East Fifth Street, a fifth-floor walk-up. There was no phone, and Woody could barely lurch down all five flights of stairs. But to Woody's intense disappointment, nobody wanted to work with him. Friends turned away, disgusted and angry, or full of pity. There wasn't a chance he could perform again. Woody began staying in the apartment, reading books, writing, and listening to his own records over and over again.

On the morning of February 22, 1954, Anneke went into labor. She calmly gathered a few things and took the bus to the hospital, where she gave birth to a baby girl, Lorina Lynn. Woody didn't manage to visit her at the hospital, but when she came home he had plastered the walls of the little apartment with sketches of babies and barely legible signs that read "Welcome Lorina Lynn."

Anneke found a secretarial job and left Lorina in Woody's care. She didn't feel good about Woody taking care of the baby, but they were so broke she couldn't hire anyone. It was the dead of winter, and Woody put pie plates over the burners of the stove and turned them on full-blast to heat up the room.

When Anneke got home the baby would be naked on the bed, a wet stain under her. Woody was often naked himself, and drunk on ale. The place was filthy. Anneke would clean up the apartment and hand wash all the diapers, lugging them up to the roof to dry when the weather was clear. She was miserable but didn't know what to do.

It was a situation ripe for explosion, and one day it came. Woody spilled some ale and grabbed a handful of clean diapers to wipe it up. Anneke yelled at him to use a rag, then

City Prison Houses Distinguished
Author And Composer--And Hobo

By EUGENE GROVE

"Saturday's child," a proverb says, "has far to go."

And Woodrow Wilson Guthrie, citizen of New York City and the world at large, surely must be a Saturday child. He has gone far in search of the Big Rock Candy Mountain.

THE JOURNEY of Woody Guthrie, successful author, successful composer, successful musician and successful hobo, however, was temporarily detoured—for the 12th time in six weeks—an enforced stay in the jail. This time, it was the Columbus City Prison.

"I don't mind," Guthrie said, gazing abstractedly out a window of the jail. "Give me a chance to get a shower and a couple meals. And they give me a suspended sentence, too.

"SOME OF THE JAILS I been, they get tough, but most places like this—if you're just passing through, the judge understands and suspends the sentence." Woody was arrested for trespassing on railroad property, held overnight for court and released.

"I was sleeping on a flat car," he said.

"On a Pennsy express I caught in East St. Louis . . ." His voice trailed off in a chuckle. "They call it their 'fast' express.

"IT'S HARD TO TELL what you can do. "Some places they throw you onto a train to get you out of town and other places, like here, they drag you off a freight to stick you in jail."

Woody paused, lit a cigaret with an awkward, stiff-handed motion. "Burned my hand in a fire in Florida last year," he explained. "They told me I'd never use it again.

"Before the officer hauled me off, a brakeman slipped me a dollar. Something like that always happens just when you get to starving.

"I CAN SAFELY SAY Americans will let you get awful hungry but they never quite let you starve."

The thin, five-foot, six-inch, 125-pounder is a hobo by avocation.

SATURDAY'S CHILD HAS FAR TO GO, a proverb says, and Woodrow Wilson Guthrie, 42, of New York, has traveled far in the past 20 years. Hobo, author and composer, Guthrie says: "I don't know why I travel . . I just feel I gotta. Daniel Boone felt that way." (Photo by Citizen Staff Photographer Lloyd Flowers)

practice.

"Same way with my albums. I get $25 a week guaranteed this year, $50 next year and $100 a week the following year. That way, there ain't so much taxes.

"I GOT ANOTHER song called 'Way Down In the Oklahoma Hills Where I Was Born.' Bob Crosby made a record of that with a lot of saxophones, but my cousin's getting all the money from it."

In the Merchant Marine during the war, Guthrie took part in the invasions of North Africa, Sicily and Normandy and was torpedoed twice. "After that, I was in the

food. The rich ones can't eat and the poor ones don't eat so it's all the same. My book, 'Bound for Glory,' was about that, about people. It was about a bunch of hoboes going around the country looking for jobs in war plants, about getting ready for war and Hitler and about racial intolerance."

(The book is in the Columbus Public Library, a library aide said, marked "special." "That's how we used to mark books that were, well, you know, off-color," she explained.)

"TELL MY WIFE when I'm leavin'?" Guthrie said. "Naw, I

A local reporter for the *Columbus Citizen* wrote an article about Woody when he passed through town, landing in the local jail. Woody pasted it into his scrapbook and scrawled "Pretty Boy Guthrie" across it.

lunged for him, trying to strangle him, and it was all Woody could do to fend her off with his twitching, shaking arms.

A few days later, Woody disappeared. He talked Ramblin' Jack into going west, and they drove all the way back to Topanga Canyon. After staying with friends for a few days, Woody asked Jack to go into town and get some food. When Jack returned with ale and hot dogs, Woody was gone.

He took off on what would be his last, wild flight across the country. Heading north he made it to Olympia, Washington, where he was arrested for vagrancy and released. He showed up next in Pampa, Texas, horrifying all his old friends and family, except for Matt Jennings, who fed him, cleaned him up, and put him on a bus back to New York.

At some point he got off the bus and turned up in Columbus, Ohio, where he was arrested again. "I don't mind," Woody told a local reporter who was delighted to find such a noted folksinger in the town jail. "Give me a chance to get a shower and a couple of meals." Released on a suspended sentence, Woody headed out the door with his only possession: *Yogi Philosophy and Oriental Occultism.*

He kept moving east, making it back to Anneke by early September. But Woody could no longer fool anyone, even himself. On September 16, 1954, he checked himself into Brooklyn State Hospital. His rambling days were over.

Chapter Thirteen
1954-1967

Windblown Seeds

"Music is just a handy way of
telling whats on your mind
No mind
No music"

This time Woody ran straight into the arms of Jesus. Every day he sat at a table in the Brooklyn State Hospital, throwing himself into his last prolific orgy of songwriting. He turned out song after song, laying himself wholeheartedly on Christ's mercy, celebrating the verses of the Bible, reveling in his faith in God.

> Christ youre still my best doctor
> Jesus youre still my best doctor
> Christ youre still my best doctor
> You can cure what ails me.

After weeks of intense songwriting, Woody finally broke through his own denial. Only forty-two years old, he faced hospitalization for the rest of his life. There was nothing the doctors could do for him. Just as his mother had, he'd slowly lose himself to the ravages of Huntington's. Month after month he'd weaken until he died, dizzy and shaking, unable to even recognize those he loved.

Unable to play music any longer, Woody, seen here listening to the Terriers in 1960, still loved to listen.

He turned to the Bible with a new desire: to find the courage to face what lay ahead.

> I buzzle into my bible,
> I read what catches my eye
> I learn just how to live and work
> I learn just how to die.

Not content to just write songs, he wrote Anneke long letters on pads of paper, napkins, paper towels, anything he could get his hands on. She came home from work to find her mailbox stuffed full of nearly illegible letters from Woody.

Despite the desperate position Woody was in, Anneke decided she would do her best by him. She rented an apartment in Coney Island near the beach and found an older couple in Queens who agreed to take Lorina for a few weeks while she sorted things out. When she finished work Friday, she'd take the subway to Brooklyn to pick up Woody, swing over to Queens to get Lorina, then they'd catch a subway home. On Sunday she reversed the trip, taking Lorina to Queens and Woody back to the hospital.

Despite Anneke's best efforts, weekends were a disaster. She'd hoped Woody would enjoy walking on the beach and being with her and Lorina. But Woody was depressed and anxious, and spent his weekends reading continuously and scribbling out songs, ignoring her and the baby.

As the weeks went by, Lorina cried and clung to her foster parents when Anneke and Woody came to pick her up. Anneke realized she couldn't keep up the pretense that they were a family. She quit arranging weekends together and decided to place Lorina in an adoption agency.

The agency informed her that because of Woody's Huntington's, Lorina would never be put up for adoption, but would remain institutionalized until she was an adult. Desperate, Anneke asked the couple in Queens to adopt Lorina. By now, they adored

Lorina, and agreed, despite their age. With her daughter taken care of, Anneke drifted further away from Woody, finally leaving New York for good.

By March 1955 Woody's songfest played itself out. One of the last songs he wrote was astonishingly simple:

> God O God O God my God
> God O God my God my God
> My God my God my God O God
> It's God my God O God O God

It was impossible to tell: Was his song an agonized cry for help, or a transcendent cry of joy, a revelation as if he had realized something: "Oh God! Oh God!"

With Anneke out of Woody's life, Marjorie stepped forward, resuming her old role of caring for him. She visited him regularly and wrote often, telling him what the children were doing and what was going on in the folk music community.

Marjorie kept her letters upbeat and full of news, but she was having her own struggles, wondering how she was going to manage financially. As Woody's fame continued to spread and his friends asked what they could do to help, she came up with a plan: Why not have a folk music concert to raise money for their three children? Early in 1956 she met with Harold Leventhal, Pete Seeger, and Lee Hays to enlist their help.

On March 17, they held the concert in Pythian Hall in New York. More than a thousand people filled the theater. The hall rang with songs performed by the Almanacs, musicians from People's Songs, and old friends and colleagues of Woody's. To close the concert, Pete Seeger gathered all the performers onstage and they sang a fervent, rousing version of "This Land Is Your Land." As the audience broke into wild cheering and clapping, the spotlight suddenly swung up to the balcony where Woody lurched to his feet and stood, soaking up their applause.

From that moment on, "This Land Is Your Land" took on a new, mythical meaning, spreading across America like windblown seeds. The Weavers, having ridden out the blacklist, transfixed a sell-out crowd in their spring concert at Carnegie Hall with "This

Land Is Your Land," and used it to lead off their third album. College students picked up the song, sang it in their dormitories, and taught it to eager young summer campers. A new generation grabbed hold of folk music, wanting to express their innermost feelings in this truthful music.

After hearing such a heartwarming tribute paid to him at Pythian Hall, Woody wasn't ready to disappear without a fight. He found he could check himself out of the hospital, and began showing up unannounced at friends' houses. People greeted him anxiously, keeping a sharp eye on him. It was one thing to sing his music in a concert hall, another to have Woody at the house, shaking and twitching, struggling to light his cigarettes, asking for platefuls of food. On one visit to Harold Leventhal's he set the couch on fire. Another day, Harold had to rush to a woman's house to rescue her from Woody, caught in one of his angry, violent moods.

Woody in Greystone Park Hospital, 1958.

Late in May Woody left the hospital, determined to head west. He managed to get on a bus but was arrested a few hours later in New Jersey when he couldn't pay the fare. Woody explained he was not drunk, but a sick man, and was taken to a nearby psychiatric hospital, Greystone Park in Morris Plains, New Jersey.

Though Woody called the new hospital Gravestone, he liked it better than Brooklyn State. The big, institutional buildings were surrounded by huge, rolling lawns, flowerbeds, and trees, and he was allowed to wander freely on the grounds.

Marjorie, afraid to bring Woody home because of his violent outbursts, brought the kids to visit him at Greystone. While she went inside to get Woody, the kids waited under a tree whose soft, full limbs reached down to the ground like a bunch of elephant trunks. The kids, now nine, eight, and six, dubbed it their "magic" tree. Marjorie brought Woody outside and spread out huge picnics, while Arlo played the harmonica and guitar for his father.

Some days they took Woody off the grounds to eat in a restaurant. Slurping and shaking, he devoured enormous amounts of food, his body burning through calories from so much constant movement. If he had to go to the bathroom, he'd throw his arm over Arlo's skinny shoulders and the two of them would weave their way to the restroom.

In December 1956 Woody's father died, and he wrote his sister Mary Jo: "I say lets not be worrie eyedy weery eyedy nor tearyful eyedy to see him passy on up to the everlovin fingers of our good good lorde and our saver there Jesus."

A few days later he wrote to Marjorie, asking her and the kids to "comey visit me in my magicy tree againe." It was his last letter. After capturing every thought, feeling, idea, and fervent political belief he had on paper, Woody could no longer control his hand enough to write.

At Greystone, Woody wasn't allowed to check himself out of the hospital. But friends came to visit, bringing candies and cookies, along with cigarettes. Just as he'd always shared whatever he had on the road, Woody broke into cigarette cartons and candy boxes as soon as he was given them, then staggered around the ward passing them out to other patients.

Two of the Weavers, Ronnie Gilbert and Fred Hellerman, came to visit Woody one day. Knowing how Woody cherished his freedom, they were upset by the locked doors and barred windows, and said it must be really hard to be there.

"No, it's okay," Woody insisted. "It's the freest place in the whole United States."

"What do you mean, Woody?" Ronnie said. "There are bars on all the windows."

"Yeah, but I can jump up on a table here and yell that I am a Communist, and nobody will arrest me. They'll just say 'he's crazy!'"

In 1959, Bob and Sid Gleason, longtime fans of Woody's living near Greystone, started bringing him to their house on Sundays. Woody was thrilled to leave the hospital. As they drove away he'd defiantly roll the windows up and down in the back seat of the car. He hated the locked windows at Greystone. At the house, he'd eat ten or twelve hot dogs at one sitting, throwing aside the buns and wolfing down the meat.

Marjorie brought the children over, preferring it to the hospital. Word spread quickly through the folk community, and the house filled with young folksingers eager to gather together and play for Woody. Old friends like Ramblin' Jack and Pete Seeger came. Everyone ate and drank, told stories, and played music together, while Woody sat on the couch, shaking and slurring his words, listening to the music.

In 1960 Cisco moved back to New York and joined the informal Sunday gatherings. He was popular at the Gleasons', not only because he was one of Woody's closest friends, but because he was such a genuinely kind and wonderful man. Cisco's career finally took off, and he toured India and performed in the second Newport Folk Festival. Around town, he was sought after at folk music nightclubs.

Thirteen-year-old Arlo snuck in the back door of the clubs to watch him perform. Because Arlo was Woody Guthrie's son they let him stay, sitting at a dimly lit table, drinking scotch, soaking up the music that Woody had helped create.

But Cisco hadn't been in New York for long when he was diagnosed with terminal stomach cancer. He decided to keep playing music while he could, and was adamant that people not feel sorry for him.

"What happened to Woody and me are just mistakes of nature, things that will someday be overcome," Cisco told Lee Hays. "That's not nearly as great a tragedy as millions of

A gathering of friends and family, 1962. Standing, from left: Arlo Guthrie, Will Geer, Cisco Houston, Lee Hays, and Millard Lampell. Seated, from left: Woody, Nora Guthrie, and Sonny Terry.

people blown to hell in a war which could be avoided. Those are the real tragedies of life."

Cisco's last performance was at Gerde's Folk City. Arlo sat at a table, watching Cisco doing his best to ignore the constant pain in his stomach, singing in his beautiful tenor. When Cisco finished, he beckoned Arlo up onto the stage.

Arlo launched into one of his father's songs, trembling with stage fright. He felt like he couldn't breathe, couldn't play the guitar, couldn't sing. But he managed a few more of Woody's songs, then leapt off the stage to encouraging applause.

A few weeks later, in February 1961, Woody was brought out of Greystone for the evening. Friends gathered at a nightclub to play music for him. Cisco came in and saw Woody sitting in a chair, shaking so badly he was having trouble staying in his seat. Lee Hays watched as Cisco walked over to Woody and kissed him on the forehead. Woody, never big on physical contact, seemed to lift up his head to be kissed. "It was a stunning moment," said Lee. In April, Cisco died.

A few months before Cisco's death, Bob Dylan had come to New York looking for Woody. Only nineteen years old, he hitchhiked from Minnesota in the dead of winter, lugging his guitar and a knapsack. He knew every song Woody had ever recorded, and had read Woody's book, *Bound for Glory*, until it was tattered and worn. Within hours of arriving in Greenwich Village, Dylan made his way to an open mike at the Cafe Wha?. He played a few songs, then announced, "I been traveling around the country. Followin' in Woody Guthrie's footsteps." He was raw, with no professional polish, but there was something charismatic about him and his music.

A day or two later Dylan hitchhiked out to Greystone to see Woody. It was a fantastic meeting for Dylan, and he sent a postcard home to friends: "I know Woody. I know Woody . . . I know him and met him and saw him and sang to him. I know Woody . . . Goddamn."

Dylan was soon one of the regulars at the Gleasons. He sat on the floor, playing his guitar and singing, listening patiently to Woody as he struggled to talk.

Woody called Dylan simply "the boy," and often asked the Gleasons if he would be showing up on Sunday. "That boy's got a voice," he said. "Maybe he won't make it with his writing, but he can sing it. He can really sing it."

Dylan spent his evenings in the nightclubs and his days practicing, weaving in everything he had seen and heard and felt. He was soon good enough to play a two-week gig at Gerde's Folk City. He opened his first set with "House of the Rising Sun" and followed up with a song he had written in a rush of enthusiasm and gratitude, "Song to Woody." In his rough, gravely voice, Dylan pledged that he would carry on in the tradition, not only of Woody, but Cisco and Sonny and Leadbelly as well.

While Dylan was finding his place in the New York folk scene, Pete Seeger was standing trial for contempt of Congress. His every move monitored by the FBI for years, he was finally convicted on ten counts of contempt for his testimony before the House Un-American Activities Committee (HUAC). In April 1961, he was sentenced to a year for every count, to be served concurrently.

Three weeks after he was released on bail, Pete played at the Village Gate. A pall hung over the audience: Would Pete soon be going to jail? Pete launched into several dozen folk songs, many of them considered subversive. His mes-

Bob Dylan, 1965.

sage was clear: The government could lock him up, but it couldn't shut him up. To wild applause, Pete finished the program with Woody's song "So Long It's Been Good to Know Yuh."

More than a year later, on May 18, 1962, the Court of Appeals dismissed his case, and Pete was free of the conviction that had been hanging over him. He and Arlo went out to the hospital to sing duets to Woody. Woody could no longer applaud, but his eyes shone with tears.

By the third annual Newport Folk Festival in 1963, more than thirty-seven thousand

Joan Baez, 1967.

people gathered to hear the concert in Rhode Island. There was an enormous array of talent, with everyone from old blues players to commercial folksingers. But the show belonged to the young protest singers—"Woody's children" as they were called in the program notes.

These earnest young musicians sent folk music whirling off in a new direction, straight into the center of the struggle for civil rights. A month later, Dylan, Odetta, Joan Baez, and dozens of other performers took part in the March on Washington. Two hundred thousand demonstrators listened to them sing and heard Martin Luther King give his eloquent speech, "I have a dream. . . . I have a dream. . . . Free at last! Free at last! Thank God Almighty, we are free at last!"

Dylan's new song "Blowin' in the Wind," swept the county. It became the most widely sung "freedom song" of the civil rights movement, and Dylan was acknowledged as the best protest singer around. It was clear: Dylan had grabbed the scepter that Woody had held defiantly overhead for so long—the ability to write and sing new folk songs honed by the political turmoil and oppression of the times.

As folk music flourished, Woody declined. His movements were larger and more erratic. His right arm was especially wild, flying up unexpectedly, sometimes hitting him right in the forehead. At times he fell into a stupor where he couldn't easily be reached.

Despite all the movement, Woody was much weaker. His attacks of rage were no longer threatening, but were more pathetic. Unable to keep his balance, he would lurch and stagger, spit running down his chin until his anger and agitation wore off. Nobody liked it, but it was part of the Huntington's. "We just dealt with it," said Arlo.

No longer afraid of his violence, Marjorie felt comfortable bringing Woody home to visit the family. After struggling out of the car, Woody would throw an arm over Arlo's shoulders and they'd make their way into the house and find a place for Woody to sit down. Beds and couches were best, so his movements wouldn't toss him onto the ground.

Riding the crest of the folk music wave, Woody's songs were being recorded all over the world in different languages. Arlo would play them for Woody on the record player, and read from the hundreds of fan letters that were arriving at the house and the hospital. Marjorie and Harold Leventhal had been careful to copyright all of Woody's songs. With the folk boom going full swing, Woody's estate was making over fifty thousand dollars per year in royalties by the mid-sixties. Finally, Marjorie didn't have to worry about money.

One day at the hospital, Woody's arm flew up and smashed against the wall behind him, fracturing his elbow. It didn't heal well, and Woody spent months in bed being fed intravenously. He never was able to walk more than a few steps on his own after that.

As he deteriorated, his visits with the family became shorter and less frequent. He rarely talked, and when he did, he was nearly impossible to understand. Marjorie would ask him to repeat himself over and over, and he would get terribly frustrated.

By 1965 Woody seemed oblivious to everything going on around him. He was unable to talk or communicate in any way, though Marjorie swore he could still answer "yes" by blinking his eyes. But other people were not so sure. Marjorie had him transferred to Creedmore State Hospital in Queens in 1966, where he could be on a smaller, quieter ward.

In the early fall of 1967, Marjorie took a new recording to Woody at the hospital: their son Arlo, singing a talking blues song he'd written about being arrested for littering in Massachusetts and how he managed to use his new criminal record to get out of the draft. Some of the words and their spinning twists and turns were gold-standard Guthrie: ". . . inspected, injected, detected, infected, neglected and selected," Arlo sang.

A few weeks later, Marjorie returned to the hospital. It was clear that the end was near. Woody lay in a hospital bed, the wild shaking and jerking of Huntington's quieted down to small shivering ripples. Marjorie leaned over and kissed him good-bye, and a priest read the Twenty-third Psalm. She knew she would never see him again.

Early the next morning, on October 3, 1967, Woody died. He was fifty-five years old. Marjorie asked that his body be cremated, and called friends with the news. Within hours, word spread coast to coast as Woody's death was announced, and "This Land Is Your Land" was played across America in tribute.

A few weeks later Marjorie was given a plain green can full of Woody's ashes. She and the kids took the can out to Coney Island, where Woody had walked along the boardwalk so many times. They stood indecisively at the edge of the water, unsure of what to do. Then in one fluid movement, Arlo threw the can out over the ocean. It splashed into the water, bobbed for a few moments, then disappeared beneath the waves.

Another Man's Done Gone

Sometimes I think I'm gonna lose my mind
But it don't look like I ever do
I loved so many people everywhere I went
Some too much, others not enough
I don't know, I may go down or up or anywhere
But I feel like this scribbling might stay
Maybe if I hadn't of seen so much hard feelings
I might not could have felt other people's
So when you think of me, if and when you do,
Just say, well, another man's done gone
Well, another man's done gone

Afterword

"There is a feeling in music and it carries you back down the road you have traveled and makes you travel it again."

The author on her family trip across America, 1963.

The summer after I finished fifth grade, my parents decided to take a road trip across America. My father bought an old 1949 Cadillac limousine and spray painted it a glittering, metallic gold. It was so big inside he built a platform across the back and threw a mattress on it. My parents piled the five of us kids and our two dogs in back, and we took off.

We zigzagged across the country, bickering and roughhousing in the back, watching America roll by. We wound our way up huge mountains, and coasted down into dry, sparkling deserts. We saw orchards loaded with swelling fruit, and endless wheat fields being worked by huge combines. In small dusty towns we pulled into gas stations. People's faces filled with surprise as they stared at our huge, glittering car, and at all of us as we tumbled out. In the evening my father found a camping place, and we made dinner, then sat around the fire dodging the smoke and swatting mosquitoes.

In late August we made it to New York City, our car unwieldy in the crowded, noisy streets, my mother nervously trying to keep track of us as we straggled along the sidewalks. After several weeks we headed down the spine of the Appalachians and swung west through the deep South, edging along the warm, wide-open waters of the Gulf of Mexico. In October we were in Colorado when my mother suddenly realized that school had started and we weren't there. She put in a call to the school district, asking them to save places for us. In early November we pulled back into town and I landed in Miss Brown's sixth-grade class.

At first Miss Brown made me nervous, with her metallic-blonde beehive hairdo and her long red nails, but she didn't mind that I'd been out crisscrossing America, and made sure I caught up with the class. She worked us hard all year, read us fascinating books, and cheered us on as we ran endless laps for President Kennedy's fitness program.

For graduation, Miss Brown decided we'd sing "This Land Is Your Land." We practiced quietly for several weeks in our classroom. A day before the ceremony, we walked two by two down to the auditorium for a dress rehearsal. Miss Brown wanted us to be perfect.

I knew we'd be perfect. I loved the song and felt good inside as I sang. "Let your voices fill the auditorium," Miss Brown said, signaling us to begin. But her bright smile quickly gave way to a frown as she listened. "Keep singing," she said, and walked in front of us, arms crossed, red-nailed fingers twitching nervously with the beat of the music, listening to each of us singing.

When she got to me, she shook her head. "No, no, no," she said. "You're off key. Stop singing. Just mouth the words."

A burning heat flooded my face. Stop singing? My warm, confident feelings crumbled to shame. I felt hot and angry inside. But I didn't say anything. Not to her, not to anyone.

The next day our class walked two by two into the packed auditorium. We filed onto the stage, the room full of an expectant hush. Miss Brown sounded a quiet note on her pitch pipe and beckoned us to begin. I stood up tall, mouthing the words, determined no one would know how bad I felt inside.

A few years ago, a friend suggested I write a biography of Woody Guthrie. Despite my lingering discomfort about "This Land Is Your Land," I was curious to learn more about this American folksinger and songwriter. As I began reading, I quickly found Woody fascinating: brilliant, restless, his life a string of tragedies, his spirit an amazing combination of anger, optimism, and sorrow.

I pored over photographs and soaked myself in his music, listening for hours every day. Soon I lived in two worlds: one was solid and concrete, full of family and friends, household chores and trips to the library; another part of me went out rambling with Woody. I began to recognize his discontent: a nervous, closed-in feeling that would send him out on the road, tramping, hitchhiking, swinging onto trains. As he moved across America, something inside him unwound and songs formed in his mind, taking shape under the wide open sky. When the loneliness got so bad it was eating a hole in his heart, he'd head for home—to his wife, a group of musicians, some place he felt connected.

Deep in researching the book, I went to the annual Woody Guthrie Free Folk Music Festival, held every July in his home town of Okemah, Oklahoma.

I loved being in the small, sunbaked town where Woody grew up, with lush grass and trees and dusty paths. I walked through the stifling hot air on dispirited Main Street and saw where Woody had carved his name in the fresh cement in front of a store, not once, but twice. On the hilly lot where his cyclone-smashed house had been, I stood and looked across town. To the east, old boomer shacks sagged in the sun. South of town, trucks and cars roared by on I-99, in a hurry to get where ever they were going, rushing past Okemah.

When the sun hit the horizon, I joined hundreds of others to sit in a rough, bumpy field, leaning against a bale of hay, listening to musicians perform on an open-air stage. As the light faded from the sky and the crows rose cawing from the fields, folksingers filled the stage: the Red Dirt Rangers, Mary Reynolds, and the Okemah Prophets.

As we left the concert that first night, a small wooden shack caught fire. Red and orange flames roared up into the sky, sparks flashing skyward in a smoky column and winking out in the stars. In my mind's eye I saw Woody's mother, Nora, standing beside her burning house, arms pinned to her sides, eyes full of desperation.

The last evening of the festival, Pete Seeger and his grandson Tao Rodriguez-Seeger came on stage with Woody's son Arlo Guthrie. Pete and Arlo took turns telling stories about Woody and singing his songs: "Union Maid," "Curly Headed Baby," and "Plane Wreck at Los Gatos."

"You all sing," said Pete, his head thrown back, his bony elbows jabbing the air as he played his banjo. A few voices around me joined in, but most sat quietly, listening to the performers. Arlo sang "Oklahoma Hills," and launched into "This Land Is Your Land."

As I heard the first lines sung out loud, I felt a sting of shame, a shadow of the miserable feeling I'd felt in sixth grade. Arlo shielded his eyes from the bright stage lights and looked out across the audience, perplexed as only a few voices made a tiny, whispery sound across the wide-open field.

"C'mon!" he said, strumming his guitar. "Sing! There's no such thing as a wrong note as long as you're singing!"

Suddenly some tight, hard place inside me flew open, and I was singing. I sang for Woody and his tender, hard-hitting songs. I sang for his friends, now long gone: Matt Jennings, Cisco, and Leadbelly. But most of all, I sang for myself and every kid who's ever been told to shut up.

"Now you're getting it," said Arlo.

On the last chorus we all jumped to our feet, laughing and clapping and singing as loud as we could, with no wrong notes.

After all the months I'd spent chasing Woody, walking where he'd walked, seeing what he saw, trying to feel what he felt, I finally understood what he was saying all along: music is for singing and feeling and hoping and knowing, not for getting right. Just like life.

Resources

Woody Guthrie Foundation and Archives

As Woody wandered the country during the 1940s and 50s, and later when he was hospitalized, his second wife, Marjorie Guthrie, collected and kept everything he wrote, drew, and recorded. It didn't matter if it was the hand-typed words to a famous song or a note scrawled on wrapping paper, she saved it all. When the collection became too large to keep comfortably in her house, Woody's manager Harold Leventhal took it into his New York office, where it eventually became the Woody Guthrie Foundation and Archives. Run by Woody's daughter Nora Guthrie, the archives have more than a thousand of his original song lyrics, dozens of notebooks and diaries, manuscripts, personal papers, hundreds of pages of artwork, audio recordings, and photographs. The goal of the archive is to preserve and perpetuate Woody's legacy and share his work with the public. They have an extensive Web site, www.woodyguthrie.org, with information, photos, and lists of Woody's publications and of recordings (both his and other artists'). They can be reached by mail at 250 West 57th Street, Suite 1218, New York, New York 10107.

Huntington's Disease

For many years the cause of Huntington's Disease, originally called Huntington's Chorea, was a mystery. Medical practitioners knew only that it ran in families, occurring with frightening regularity in the children of Huntington's sufferers. Then, in 1993 an American researcher, Dr. Nancy Wexler, discovered the gene responsible for Huntington's. Her discovery made it possible to use a simple blood test to see if someone would develop the disease. While the test has provided information and relief to many, it has also brought up ethical and moral dilemmas. Would you want to know if you were going to develop Huntington's later in life? If you already had children, would you have them tested, and would you tell them the results?

Today the symptoms of Huntington's can be managed more effectively than in Woody's time, but there is still no cure. Huntington's typically begins in mid-life, and after a prolonged period of degeneration, is always fatal. In the United States there are about 30,000 people with Huntington's. Two of Woody's children, Teeny and Sue, developed Huntington's and died. (Two of his other children, Bill and Lorina Lynn, were tragically killed in car accidents.) Woody's surviving children with Marjorie—Arlo, Joady, and Nora—appear to be free of the disease, although only Joady has taken the blood test.

After Woody's death, Marjorie Guthrie started the Committee to Combat Huntington's Disease. Today, the Huntington's Disease Society of America (HDSA) continues the work that she began.

For information on Huntington's Disease, you can contact the HDSA at www.hdsa.org. For information on other hereditary diseases, including Huntington's, contact the Hereditary Disease Society at www.hdfoundation.org.

Acknowledgments

This book would not have been possible without the full help and cooperation of the Woody Guthrie Archives. Nora Guthrie immediately understood what I was trying to do and gave me her whole-hearted support, as did Jorge Arevalo, Harold and Natalie Leventhal, and the enthusiastic staff.

For inspiration, encouragement and flat-out hard work I am grateful to my editor, Jill Davis. My thanks to the many people at Viking who helped this project come together: Denise Cronin, Catherine Frank, Regina Hayes, Ed Miller, John Vasile, and most especially Janet Pascal for her thoughtful work, and Lane Smith for the beautiful, wacky cover.

My thanks to Pete Seeger for generously sharing his memories, thoughts, and feelings about Woody, and for carefully reading the manuscript and making insightful comments. I'm grateful also to Arlo Guthrie who talked deeply and honestly about his father, and Joe Klein, who interviewed many of Woody's friends and colleagues in the late 1970s for his book *Woody Guthrie: A Life*, then donated the tapes to the Woody Guthrie Archives. Many of those interviewed are no longer living, and listening to their stories enriched my understanding of Woody and his times.

In putting together images for the book I was especially helped by Seema Weatherwax, Rondal Partridge, Patricia Lowe at the Will Rogers Memorial and Birthplace, Juanita Householder at Highlander Research and Educational Center, and Stephanie Smith and Jeff Place at the Center for Folklife and Cultural Heritage at the Smithsonian Institution.

Finally, my gratitude to my writer friends who patiently offered suggestions: Susan Campbell Bartoletti, Bill Broder, Alla Crone, Dan Davis, Anna Grossnickle Hines, Gary Hines, Ella Ellis, Meg Partridge, Zilpha Keatley Snyder, and Martha Weston, as well as my intrepid agent, Ruth Cohen.

Source Notes

General Sources

With someone as prolific as Woody Guthrie it's hard to believe that his creative life span was just over twenty years, from the time he was a young adult in Texas in the mid-1930s, until the mid-1950s, when Huntington's Disease closed in on him. Yet during those two decades he wrote more than three thousand songs, filled dozens of journals, and wrote thousands of letters and two autobiographies.

For the flavor of Woody's life according to Woody see his autobiographies, *Bound for Glory*, and *Seeds of Man: An Experience Lived and Dreamed*. (Many people consider them "semi-autobiographical," particularly *Seeds of Man*, because Woody was known to stretch the truth when it suited him.) For a good overview of his shorter writings, see *Pastures of Plenty: A Self-Portrait*.

The hundreds of songs that Woody recorded in his lifetime have been released and re-released many times. Smithsonian Folkways Recordings has a number of CDs and tapes available at www.si.edu/folkways. For the most thorough listing of his music see *Hard Travelin': The Life and Legacy of Woody Guthrie*, edited by Robert Santelli and Emily Davidson.

There have also been a number of wonderful, detailed books published about Woody and his times. My favorites are *Woody Guthrie: A Life* by Joe Klein, *Woody, Cisco and Me: Seamen Three in the Merchant Marine* by Vincent "Jim" Longhi, and *Woody Guthrie and Me: An Intimate Reminiscence* by Edward Robbin.

If you can find a copy of *Woody Guthrie Folk Songs: A Collection of Songs by America's Foremost Balladeer* at your library you will find the music and words to several hundred of Woody's original songs. More widely available is *Hard Hitting Songs for Hard-Hit People* compiled by Alan Lomax, with songs by Woody and other folk songs of the Depression, and notes on each song by Woody.

Chapter Sources

To streamline Woody's more rambling quotations I sometimes left out words without adding ellipses. His unique spelling and punctuation, however, I left intact. As I compiled the footnotes I took the liberty of not using double quotation marks when quoting dialog from a book.

Front matter

"Woody spent his life . . .": *A Tribute to Woody Guthrie*, CD liner notes by Millard Lampell (Warner Brothers Records Inc. CD 9 26036-2, 1972), p. 9.

Preface: Ramblin 'Round

"I hate a song . . .": *A Tribute to Woody Guthrie*, cut 17.

"I had rather sound . . .": Woody Guthrie Archives, New York, N.Y., Mss. 2, Box 1, Folder 35.

"All you can write . . .": Woody Guthrie, *Pastures of Plenty: A Self Portrait*, edited by David March and Harold Leventhal (New York: Harper Collins, 1990), p. xxiv.

"That shows . . .": Pete Seeger, Tribute in *This Land Is Your Land* by Woody Guthrie, illustrated by Kathy Jakobsen (Boston: Little Brown and Company, 1998), unpaginated (overflap).

"one guitar picker . . .": Ibid.

"hundreds of millions . . .": Ibid.

"I am out . . .": *A Tribute to Woody Guthrie*, cut 17.

Chapter One: Insane-Asylum Baby

"Don't you never . . .": *A Tribute to Woody Guthrie*, cut 26.

"long and sad . . .": Guthrie, *Pastures of Plenty*, p. 177.

"Whattaya know . . .": Woody Guthrie, *Bound for Glory* (New York: Plume, an imprint of Dutton Signet, 1983), p. 81.

"As long as . . .": Joe Klein, *Woody Guthrie: A Life* (New York: Dell Publishing, a Division of Random House, 1999), p. 2.

"It is generally thought . . .": Ibid., p. 10.

"sticking her head . . .": Alan Lomax, comp. *Hard Hitting Songs for Hard-Hit People*, notes on the songs by Woody Guthrie, music transcribed and edited by Pete Seeger (New York: Oak Publications 1967), p. 334.

"happy as a lobster.": Klein, *Woody Guthrie*, p. 14.

"You are . . .": Guthrie, *Bound for Glory*, p. 55.

"The color . . .": Woody Guthrie Archives, *My Life*, typed ms.

Listen to the music . . .: Guthrie, *Bound for Glory*, p. 38.

"outwit, outsmart . . .": Ibid., p. 39.

"The songs . . .": Woody Guthrie Archives, *My Life*, typed ms.

"I'm a-gonna run . . .": Guthrie, *Bound for Glory*, p. 84.

You could see . . .: Ibid., p. 88.

"coal oil lights . . ." Woody Guthrie Archives, Song Folders.

"Hello there . . .": Guthrie, *Bound for Glory*, p. 134.

"Did I pass?": *A Tribute to Woody Guthrie*, cut 26.

Chapter Two: Boomtown

"I guess I hoped . . .": Woody Guthrie Archives, Corr. 1, Box 1, Folder 44.

"It was too much . . .": Guthrie, *Pastures of Plenty*, p. 3.

"God, I want . . .": Guthrie, *Bound for Glory*, p. 135.

Stewbally is a good horse . . .: Woody Guthrie Archives, Mss. 2, Box 1, Folder 35.

"Just like you . . .": Guthrie, *Bound for Glory*, p. 139.

"Maybe you don't . . .": Ibid., p 150.

"struck a million . . .": Ibid.

"feeling a new . . .": Ibid., p 149.

"There was a feeling . . .": Ibid., p 153.

"My ancestors . . .": Bryan Sterling, *The Best of Will Rogers* (New York: Crown Publishers, 1979), p. 180.

"Where . . .": Guthrie, *Bound for Glory*, p. 157.

"That house . . .": Ibid., p 158.

"That's the lonesomest . . .": *Woody Guthrie: Library of Congress Recordings*, recorded by Alan Lomax, Rounder CD, 1041/2/3, 1988, Cambridge Mass., disc 1, cut 2.

"You're Woodrow . . .": Matt Jennings, interview by Joe Klein, Woody Guthrie Archives.

Chapter Three: Dusty Old Dust

"Us Okies . . .": Guthrie, *Pastures of Plenty*, p. 38.

"the right bed . . .": Woody Guthrie Archives, Mss. 2, Box 1, Folder 34.

"It was hot . . .": Guthrie, *Bound for Glory*, p. 173.

"They shall lay hands . . .": Mark 16:18.

"You can't . . .": Ben Yagoda, *Will Rogers: A Biography* (New York: Alfred Knopf, 1993), p. 295.

"He swallowed . . .": Ibid., p. 303.

"You don't want . . .": Klein, *Woody Guthrie*, p. 61.

"The lust for comfort . . .": Kahlil Gibran, *The Prophet*, reprinted online at www.cc.columbia.edu/~gm84/gibtable.

"All kinds of cars . . .": Guthrie, *Bound for Glory*, p. 188.

"The prayer of faith . . .": James 5:14-15.

"The deeper . . .": Gilbran, *The Prophet*.

"Things was starting . . .": Guthrie, *Bound for Glory*, p. 177.

"Some people liked me . . .": Ibid., p. 178

"A whole bunch of us . . .": *Woody Guthrie: Library of Congress Recordings*, disc 1, cut 8.

"So long . . .": Ibid.

"dusted us over . . .": Ibid.

So long . . .: Ibid., disc 1, cut 9.

Chapter Four: California and Lefty Lou

"Days tried to thumb . . .": Lomax, *Hard Hitting Songs for Hard-Hit People*, p. 23.

She's my Curly . . .: Woody Guthrie, *Woody Guthrie Folk Songs* (New York: Ludlow Music Inc., 1963), p. 57.

"You didn't know . . .": Woody Guthrie, *Woody Sez*, compiled and edited by Marjorie Guthrie, Harold Leventhal, Terry Sullivan, and Sheldon Patinkin (New York: Grosset & Dunlap, 1975), p. 83.

"All you have . . .": Guthrie, *Bound for Glory*, p. 223.

"Lefty Lou . . .": Klein, *Woody Guthrie*, p. 91.

Dear Mother . . .: Guthrie, *Pastures of Plenty*, p. 19.

"'Folks,' he said . . .": Pete Seeger, interview by Elizabeth Partridge, New York, May 17, 2000.

California is a garden . . .: Guthrie, *Woody Guthrie Folk Songs*, p. 66.

"I was born . . .": Klein, *Woody Guthrie*, p. 99.

Way down yonder . . .: *A Tribute to Woody Guthrie*, cut 3.

Chapter Five: "Woody Sez"

"The best stuff you can sing . . .": Guthrie, *Pastures of Plenty*, p. 49.

"I still feel . . .": Woody Guthrie Archives, Song Folders.

"damn bankers . . .": Ed Robbin, *Woody Guthrie and Me: An Intimate Reminiscence* (Berkeley, Calif: Lancaster-Miller Publishers), p. 31.

"I would like . . .": Ibid., p. 32.

"Where ya been?": Ibid., p. 35.

"I'd like to see . . .": Ibid., p. 36.

"Billionaires cause hoboes . . .": Guthrie, *Woody Sez*, p. 37.

"Just traveling around . . .": Klein, *Woody Guthrie*, p. 114.

This world . . .: Ibid., p. 119.

"lived outside . . .": *Woody Guthrie: Library of Congress Recordings*, disc 2, cut 5.

"I spoke out . . .": Woody Guthrie Archives, Mss. 2, Box 1, Folder 34.

"So we drove . . .": Ibid.

"Now it looks . . .": Woody Guthrie Archives Corr. 1, Box 1, Folder 14.

"Special to . . .": Guthrie, *Woody Sez*, p. 40.

"frozen stiff . . .": Woody Guthrie Archives, Mss. 2, Box 1, Folder 34.

"I will never forget . . .": Ibid.

"Guys passed out . . .": Guthrie, *Woody Sez*, p. 55.

"I didn't know . . .": Ibid., p. 54.

Chapter Six: Hitting the Big Time

"With all these poor . . .": *Woody Guthrie: Library of Congress Recordings*, unpaginated liner notes by Alan Lomax.

"All you can write . . .": Guthrie, *Pastures of Plenty*, p. xxiv.

"I saw how the poor . . .": Jeff Place and Guy Logsdon, comps, *The Asch Recordings* (Washington, D.C.: Smithsonian Folkways, 1997), vol. 1, liner notes pp. 17-18.

"It ain't just . . .": Woody Guthrie Archives, Song Folders.

"I don't want . . .": *Woody Guthrie: Library of Congress Recordings*, unpaginated liner notes by Alan Lomax.

"I've always . . .": Ibid, disc 1, cut 5.

"I never did . . .": Ibid.

"Have you . . .": Pete Seeger, interview by Elizabeth Partridge, New York, October 1, 2001.

"I can't make . . .": David King Dunaway, *How Can I Keep from Singing: Pete Seeger* (New York: McGraw-Hill, 1981), p. 65.

"In the Blue Ridge . . .": *Woody Guthrie: Library of Congress Recordings*, unpaginated liner notes by Alan Lomax.

"Sooner or later . . .": Pete Seeger, interview by Elizabeth Partridge, New York, May 17, 2000.

There once . . .: Guthrie, *Woody Guthrie Folk Songs*, p. 94.

"Is that . . .": Pete Seeger, *The Incompleat Folksinger* (New York: Simon and Schuster, 1972), p. 56.

"Lord, lord . . .": Ibid.

"You've got to . . .": Pete Seeger, interview by Elizabeth Partridge, New York, May 17, 2000.

"The blues is . . .": Charles Wolfe and Kip Lornell, *The Life and Legend of Leadbelly* (New York: Da Capo Press, 1999), p. 218.

"He had . . .": Ibid., pp. 217-18.

"They are . . .": Klein, *Woody Guthrie*, p. 174.

"They called me . . .": Ibid., p. 175.

"All them white . . .": Will Geer, interview by Joe Klein, Woody Guthrie Archives.

Chapter Seven: On the Road Again

"I have always . . .": Woody Guthrie Archives, Corr. 1, Box 1, Folder 44.

"You mean . . .": Robbin, *Woody Guthrie and Me*, p. 59.

"On more . . .": Guthrie, *Pastures of Plenty*, p. 54.

"I want . . .": Seema Weatherwax, interview by Elizabeth Partridge, Santa Cruz, Calif., August 10, 1999.

"Today is lonesome . . .": Klein, *Woody Guthrie*, p. 187.

"hated all . . .": Guthrie, *Pastures of Plenty*, p. 69.

Well it's always . . .: *A Tribute to Woody Guthrie*, cut 11.

"full of guts . . .": Willens, Doris, *Lonesome Traveler: The Life of Lee Hays* (New York: W. W. Norton, 1988), p. 67.

"Well, I guess . . .": Pete Seeger, interview by Elizabeth Partridge, New York, May 17, 2000.

"Our whole politics . . .": Willens, *Lonesome Traveler*, p. 69.

"extremely untidy . . .": Dunaway, *How Can I Keep from Singing*, p. 87.

"After going . . .": Ibid., pp. 87-88.

"Neither one of us . . .": Guthrie, *Pastures of Plenty*, p.70.

"You want . . .": Robbin, *Woody Guthrie and Me*, p. 89.

"I think . . .": Woody Guthrie Archives, Corr. 1, Box 1, Folder 44.

"Our deal was . . .": *Sing Out! The Folk Song Magazine*, vol. 40 no. 3, Nov./Dec. 1995 /Jan. 1996, p. 43.

"they were playing . . .": Ibid., p. 44.

"I know . . .": Wolfe, *The Life and Legend of Leadbelly*, p. 227.

"If a white man . . .": *Sing Out!* p. 44.

I went . . .: Pete Seeger, interview by Elizabeth Partridge, New York, October 1, 2001.

"Let's win . . .": Pete Seeger, interview by Elizabeth Partridge, New York, May 17, 2000.

Chapter Eight: Folksay Dancers

"I am stormy . . ."; Guthrie, *Pastures of Plenty*, p. 104.

"I'm coming . . .": Marjorie Guthrie, interview by Joe Klein, Woody Guthrie Archives,

"Wherever little kids . . ." Seeger, *The Incompleat Folksinger*, p. 47.

"fume and cuss . . .": Woody Guthrie Archives, Corr. 1, Box 1, Folder 43.

"If I want . . .": Klein, *Woody Guthrie*, p. 231.

"awful friendly . . .": Woody Guthrie Archives, Corr. 1 Box 1, Folder 43.

"We had . . .": Ibid.

"I'll always believe . . .": Ibid.

"I'm goin' . . .": Klein, *Woody Guthrie*, p. 236.

"They widen out . . .": Woody Guthrie Archives, Corr. 1 Box 1, Folder 43.

"I think I fell . . .": Ibid.

"I didn't want . . .": Ibid.

"12 of the most . . .": Ibid.

"The movement . . .": Ibid.

"I saved up . . .": Ibid.

"sings . . .": Ibid.

"Imagine us . . .": Ibid.

"I have dreams . . .": Klein, *Woody Guthrie*, p. 248.

"There are red devils . . .": Woody Guthrie Archives, Corr. 1 Box 1, Folder 43.

"Didn't you see me . . ." *Sing Out!* p. 44.

"Me and Sonny . . .": Ibid.

"Goddamn fascists! . . .": Pete Seeger, interview by Elizabeth Partridge, New York, May 17, 2000.

"I would give . . .": Woody Guthrie Archives, Corr. 1 Box 1, Folder 44.

"I have been . . .": Klein, *Woody Guthrie*, pp. 263-64.

"I FELT LIKE . . .": Ibid., p. 265.

"many times . . .": Woody Guthrie Archives, Corr. 1 Box 1, Folder 46.

"To me people . . .": Ibid.

"I am self sufficient . . .": Klein, *Woody Guthrie*, p. 269.

"(Hello)...": Woody Guthrie Archives, Corr. 1 Box 1, Folder 46.

Chapter Nine: Shipping Out

"A torpedo knocks . . .": Guthrie, *Pastures of Plenty*, p. 87.

"Aunt Jenny's . . .": Klein, *Woody Guthrie*, p. 278.

"A ship's hit,": Longhi, Vincent "Jim." *Woody, Cisco and Me* (Champaign: University of Illinois Press 1996), p. 60.

"No, I wasn't . . .": Ibid., p. 62.

"But I'm sure . . ." Ibid.

"She held her eyes . . ." Guthrie, *Pastures of Plenty*, p. 128.

"She has come . . .": Ibid.

"I write . . .": Woody Guthrie Archives, Corr. 1, Box 1, Folder 49.

"I'm Woody . . .": Place, *The Asch Recordings*, Vol. 3, liner notes, p. 14.

"The simplicity . . .": Ibid.

"Sonny Terry . . .": Guthrie, *Pastures of Plenty*, pp. 11-12.

"a seabag . . .": Place, *The Asch Recordings*, Vol. 3, liner notes, p. 12.

"Holy Mother,": Longhi, *Woody, Cisco and Me*, p. 229.

"It's a cheerful . . .": Ibid.

"You guys . . .": Ibid.

"That's about . . .": Ibid., p. 231.

"Well, then . . .": Ibid.

The armed forces . . .: *San Francisco Chronicle*, Thursday, July 13, 2000, p. A15.

"Drunk once . . .": Arlo Guthrie, interview by Elizabeth Partridge, Okemah, Oklahoma, July 14, 2000.

Such a terrible sight . . .: Guthrie, *Woody Guthrie Folk Songs*, p. 101.

"These terrible . . ." Klein, *Woody Guthrie*, p. 307.

"It seems like . . .": Ibid., pp. 313-14.

"Just dizzy,": Woody Guthrie Archive, Corr. 1, Box 2, Folder 11.

Chapter Ten: Stackybones

"And the things . . .": Klein, *Woody Guthrie*, p. 350.

"hundreds, thousands . . .": Dunaway, *How Can I Keep from Singing*, p. 117.

"The people . . .": Klein, *Woody Guthrie*, p. 329.

"electric surge . . .": Guthrie, *Pastures of Plenty*, p. 174

Past my wing . . .: Woody Guthrie Archives, Song Folders.

"I don't know . . .": Ibid.

"an Iron Curtain . . .": Carol L. Thompson, "Sir Winston Churchill," *The World Book Encyclopedia* (Chicago, Illinois: World Book Inc., 1988), C-Ch. p. 549.

"I've been drinking . . .": Henrietta Yurchenco, assisted by Marjorie Guthrie, *A Mighty Hard Road: The Woody Guthrie Story* (New York: McGraw-Hill, 1970), p. 132.

"I feel now . . .": Klein, *Woody Guthrie*, p. 343-44.

"I have always . . .": Ibid., p. 341.

"I've been . . .": Guthrie, *Pastures of Plenty*, p. 177.

Why oh why . . .: Guthrie, *Woody Guthrie Folk Songs*, p. 55.

You stick out . . .: Woody Guthrie Archives, Song Folders.

"I'm drunk . . .": Klein, *Woody Guthrie*, p. 327.

"new baby . . .": Woody Guthrie Archives, Mss. 1, Box 4, Folder 59.

"Come to . . .": Ibid.

"I don't want . . .": Klein, *Woody Guthrie*, p. 350.

"And the things . . .": Ibid.

Chapter Eleven: Alcohol and Fists

"You've found . . .": Guthrie, *Pastures of Plenty*, p. xix.

"Cathy . . .": Woody Guthrie Archives, Corr. 1, Box 1, Folder 14.

"I just hope . . .": Woody Guthrie Archives, Mss. 1, Box 4, Folder 52.

"Homesick . . .": Woody Guthrie Archives, Corr. 1, Box 2, Folder 12.

"Oh, Daddy . . .": Klein, *Woody Guthrie*, p. 353.

"There is some . . .": Woody Guthrie Archives, Notebooks 52.

"Today I slammed . . .": Woody Guthrie Archives, Notebooks 57.

"I am soft . . .": Ibid.

"It cut me . . .": *The Worker* magazine, January 18, 1948.

Good-bye . . .: Guthrie, *Woody Guthrie Folk Songs*, p. 24.

"If these letters . . .": Klein, *Woody Guthrie*, p. 369.

"I stumbled . . .": Woody Guthrie Archives, Corr. 1, Box 3 Folder 1.

"Take it easy . . .": Woody Guthrie Archives, Song Folders.

"Let me walk . . .": Wolfe, *The Life and Legend of Leadbelly*, p. 254.

"Could have been . . .": Klein, *Woody Guthrie*, p. 365.

"Out with Ingrid . . .": Guthrie, *Pastures of Plenty*, p. 188.

Ingrid Bergman . . .: Woody Guthrie Archives, Song Folders.

"You can steal . . .": *The Ballad of Ramblin' Jack*, documentary film directed by Aiyana Elliot, written by Aiyana Elliot and Dick Dahl, 2000.

"I'll spend . . .": Klein, *Woody Guthrie*, p. 387.

"Please come back . . .": Woody Guthrie Archives, Corr. 1, Box 3, Folder 3.

"All . . .": Pete Seeger at the Woody Guthrie Free Folk Music Festival, Okemah, Oklahoma, July 15, 2000.

"I wish . . .": Klein, *Woody Guthrie*, 385.

"I'll never lose . . .": Woody Guthrie Archives, Kings County Hospital Writings, Box 7, Folder 39.

"Here's my . . .": Klein, *Woody Guthrie*, p. 395.

"PSYCHOSIS . . .": Woody Guthrie Archives, Papers, Box 2, Folder 9.

"Face seems . . .": Klein, *Woody Guthrie*, p. 397.

"Ultimate prognosis . . .": Woody Guthrie Archives, Papers, Box 2, Folder 9.

Chapter Twelve: Last Run for Freedom

"I want to rest . . .": Woody Guthrie Archives, Song Folders.

"We had started . . .": Dunaway, *How Can I Keep from Singing*, p.156.

I stumble . . .: Woody Guthrie Archives, Song Folders.

"It will all wear off . . .": Klein, *Woody Guthrie*, p. 403.

He asked . . .: Pete Seeger, interview by Elizabeth Partridge, New York, May 17, 2000.

"Power, power . . .": Seeger, *The Incompleat Folksinger*, p. 313.

"The patient . . .": Klein, *Woody Guthrie*, p. 412.

"When are you . . .": Woody Guthrie Archives, Corr. 2 Box 2, Folder 36.

"Woody, I love you . . .": Ibid.

"I don't mind . . .": Woody Guthrie Archives, Scrapbooks, Box 6.

Chapter Thirteen: Windblown Seeds

"Music is just . . .": Woody Guthrie Archives, Scrapbooks, Box 3.

Christ youre . . .: Woody Guthrie Archives, Song Folders.

I buzzle . . .: Ibid.

God O God . . .: Ibid.

"I say lets . . .": Klein, *Woody Guthrie*, p. 437.

"comey visit . . .": Ibid., p. 438.

"No, it's OK,": Pete Seeger at the Woody Guthrie Free Folk Music Festival, Okemah, Oklahoma, July 15, 2000.

"What happened . . .": Longhi, *Woody, Cisco and Me*, p. 273–74.

"It was . . .": Klein, *Woody Guthrie*, p. 449.

"I been traveling . . .": Scaduto, Anthony, *Bob Dylan: An Intimate Biography* (New York: Grosset and Dunlap, 1971), p. 52.

"I know Woody . . .": Ibid., p,. 53.

"That boy's . . .": Ibid., p. 56.

"I have a dream . . .": Ibid., p. 151.

"We just . . .": Arlo Guthrie, interview by Elizabeth Partridge, Okemah, Oklahoma, July 14, 2000.

"inspected . . .": Klein, *Woody Guthrie*, p. 464–65.

Another Man's . . .: Woody Guthrie Archives, Song Folders.

Afterword

"There is a feeling . . ." Guthrie, *Pastures of Plenty*, p. 105.

Bibliography

The Ballad of Ramblin' Jack. Documentary film by Aiyana Elliot, written by Aiyana Elliot and Dick Dahl. 2000.

Dunaway, David King. *How Can I Keep from Singing: Pete Seeger.* New York: McGraw-Hill, 1981.

Guthrie, Arlo. Interview by Elizabeth Partridge. Okemah, Oklahoma, July 14, 2000.

Guthrie, Woody. *Bound for Glory.* New York: Dutton, 1943. Reprint, New York: Plume, an imprint of Dutton Signet, 1983.

Guthrie, Woody. *Pastures of Plenty.* Edited by David March and Harold Leventhal. New York: Harper Collins, 1990.

Guthrie, Woody. *Seeds of Man: An Experience Lived and Dreamed.* New York: Dutton, 1976.

Guthrie, Woody. *This Land Is Your Land.* Introduction by Pete Seeger. Boston: Little Brown and Company, 1998.

Guthrie, Woody. *Woody Guthrie Folk Songs: A Collection of Songs by America's Foremost Balladeer.* New York: Ludlow Music, 1963.

Guthrie, Woody. *Woody Guthrie: Library of Congress Recordings.* Recorded by Alan Lomax. Rounder CD 1041/2/3. Cambridge, Mass., 1988.

Guthrie, Woody. *Woody Sez.* Compiled and edited by Marjorie Guthrie, Harold Leventhal, Terry Sullivan, and Sheldon Patinkin. New York: Grosset & Dunlap, 1975.

Klein, Joe. *Woody Guthrie: A Life.* New York: Knopf, 1980. Reprint, New York: Dell Publishing, a Division of Random House, 1999.

Lomax, Alan, comp. *Hard Hitting Songs for Hard-Hit People.* Notes on the songs by Woody Guthrie. Music transcribed and edited by Pete Seeger. New York: Oak Publications, 1967.

Longhi, Vincent "Jim." *Woody, Cisco and Me: Seamen Three in the Merchant Marine.* Champaign: University of Illinois Press, 1996.

McKinney, Larry. Interview by Elizabeth Partridge. Okemah, Oklahoma, July 15, 2000.

Place, Jeff, and Guy Logsdon, compilers. *The Asch Recordings*, Washington, D.C.: Smithsonian Folkways, 1997.

Robbin, Ed. *Woody Guthrie and Me: An Intimate Reminiscence.* Berkeley, Calif.: Lancaster-Miller Publishers, 1979.

Santelli, Robert, and Emily Davidson. *Hard Travelin': The Life and Legacy of Woody Guthrie.* Hanover, N.H.: University Press of New England, 1999.

Scaduto, Anthony. *Bob Dylan: An Intimate Biography.* New York: Grosset and Dunlap 1971.

Seeger, Pete. *The Incompleat Folksinger.* New York: Simon and Schuster, 1972.

Seeger, Pete. Interview by Elizabeth Partridge. New York, May 17, 2000.

Sing Out! The Folk Song Magazine. Vol. 40, no. 3. Nov./Dec. 1995/Jan. 1996.

Sterling, Bryan. *The Best of Will Rogers.* New York: Crown Publishers, 1979.

A Tribute to Woody Guthrie. CD liner notes by Millard Lampell. Warner Brothers Records Inc. CD 9 26036-2, 1972.

Weatherwax, Seema. Interview by Elizabeth Partridge. Santa Cruz, Calif., August 10, 1999.

Willens, Doris. *Lonesome Traveler: The Life of Lee Hays.* New York: W. W. Norton, 1988.

Wolfe, Charles, and Kip Lornell. *The Life and Legend of Leadbelly.* New York: Da Capo Press, 1999.

Yagoda, Ben. *Will Rogers: A Biography.* New York: Alfred Knopf, 1993.

Yurchenco, Henrietta, assisted by Marjorie Guthrie. *A Mighty Hard Road: The Woody Guthrie Story.* New York: McGraw-Hill, 1970.

Index

Note: Page numbers in italics indicate photographs or drawings.

Picture Credits

Bettmann/Corbis, p. 107. John Cohen, p. 186. Photograph by Leo Lieb, courtesy of Culver Pictures, Inc., p. 115. Chicago Historical Society, courtesy of Stephen Deutch, p. 94. Hulton Archive, all contents copyright 2001 Getty Images, pp. 39, 78, 93; Archive Photos, 80. Photo by Lester Balog, print by Ken Light, courtesy of Ken Light, p. 148. Harry Lasker Memorial Library and Resource Center at the Highlander Research and Educational Center, pp. 90, 91. Courtesy of the Library of Congress: Farm Security Administration-Office of War Information Collection; Dorothea Lange, p. iii (LC-USF34-002394-E), p. 51 (LC-USF34-018262-C), p. 56 (LC-USF34-016317-E), p. 57 (LC-USF34-020317-E), p. 68 (LC-USF34-018401E), p. 73 (LC-USF34-020392-C); Russell Lee, p. 20 (LC-USF33-012178-M1); Arthur Rothstein, p. 29 (LC-USF33-002831-M4), p. 50 (LC-USF34-004052): New York World-Telegram and Sun Newspaper Photograph Collection; p. 77 (LC-USZ62-120202), p. 82 (LC-USZ62-107998); photo by Al Aumuller, p. 127 (LC-USZ62-113276), p. 195 (LC-USZ62-107999), p. 196 (LC-USZ62-115876). Rondal Partridge, pp. 165, 179, 200. Courtesy of the Ralph Rinzler Archives and Collections, Center for Folklife and Cultural Heritage, Smithsonian Institution, pp. 10, 46; photos by Robert C. Malone, pp. 109, 169. Courtesy of Seema Weatherwax, Department of Special Collections, Stanford University Library, pp. vi, 100, 103, 104. Will Rogers Memorial and Birthplace, pp. 26, 43. Courtesy of the Woody Guthrie Foundation and Archives, New York, pp. 3, 4, 7, 9, 11, 14, 18, 22, 30, 32, 34, 35, 41, 45, 52, 55, 60, 65, 66, 85, 87, 88, 96, 102, 111, 112, 113, 118, 122 (bottom), 125, 126, 129, 131, 134 (top and bottom), 138, 143, 146, 153, 154 (top and bottom), 155, 161, 163, 167, 176, 180, 184, 199, endpapers. Courtesy of the Woody Guthrie Foundation and Archives and specific photographers, p. 122 (top), David Lintow; p. 158, Sid Grossman; p. 171, Robert Wersan; p. 190, Louis Gordon; p. 193, David Gahr.

Permissions

"Another Man's Done Gone," "California Stars," "Ingrid Bergman," words by Woody Guthrie. © copyright 1998 by Woody Guthrie Publications, Inc. All rights reserved. Used by permission. "Chicken Sneeze," New words and new music adaptation by Woody Guthrie. TRO—© Copyright 1963 (Renewed) Ludlow Music, Inc., New York, NY. Used by permission. "Curly Headed Baby," words and music by Woody Guthrie. TRO—© copyright 1961 (Renewed) 1963 (Renewed) 1977 Ludlow Music, Inc., New York, NY. Used by permission. "Do Re Mi," "Howdido," "Union Maid," words and music by Woody Guthrie. TRO—© copyright 1961 (Renewed) 1963 (Renewed) Ludlow Music, Inc., New York, NY. Used by permission. "God O God," "I Ain't Dead," "Jesus My Doctor," "Kiss My Mother Again," "My Reddy Paint Bible," words by Woody Guthrie. © copyright 2001 by Woody Guthrie Publications, Inc. All rights reserved. Used by permission. "Greenback Dollar" (Greenback Money), words and music by Woody Guthrie. TRO—© copyright 2001 Ludlow Music, Inc. Used by permission. "I Ain't Got No Home," words and music by Woody Guthrie. TRO—© copyright 1961 (Renewed) 1964 (Renewed) Ludlow Music, Inc., New York, NY. Used by permission. "Oklahoma Hills" by Woody Guthrie and Jack Guthrie. Copyright © 1945—Renewed 1973 Michael H. Goldsen, Inc. Used by Permission. International Copyright Secured. All Rights Reserved. "Pastures of Plenty," "Tom Joad," words and music by Woody Guthrie. TRO—© copyright 1960 (Renewed) 1963 (Renewed) Ludlow Music, Inc., New York, NY. Used by permission. "Plane Wreck at Los Gatos (Deportee)," words by Woody Guthrie; music by Martin Hoffman. TRO—© copyright 1961 (Renewed) 1963 (Renewed) Ludlow Music, Inc. New York, NY. Used by permission. "So Long It's Been Good to Know Yuh" (Dusty Old Dust), words and music by Woody Guthrie. TRO—© copyright 1940 (Renewed) 1950 (Renewed) 1963 (Renewed) Folkways Music Publishers, Inc., New York, NY. Used by permission. "This Land Is Your Land," words and music by Woody Guthrie. TRO—© copyright 1956 (Renewed) 1958 (Renewed) 1970 (Renewed) Ludlow Music, Inc., New York, NY. Used by permission. "Why Oh Why," words and music by Woody Guthrie. TRO—© copyright 1960 (Renewed) 1963 (Renewed) 1972 Ludlow Music, Inc. Used by permission. *Time*, April 15, 1946 © Time Inc. Reprinted by permission. All original Woody Guthrie quotes are copyrighted by Woody Guthrie Publications, Inc. and are used by permission. All rights reserved.